FUN ON THE MERRY-GO-ROUND WITH A SIXPENCE TO SPEND.

THERESA J. SEARLE

In the loving memory of my parents, Violet & Albert, who will never be forgotten.

Acknowledgements

I would like to say a thank you to my family for all of their support and encouragement over the past few years I have been writing my book.

My husband Clive, son and daughter Sharon & Adam and my grandchildren James & Emily.

Also a thank you to Gary Dalkin, Steven Baker and to the Molesey History Society for giving their kind permission in allowing me to use their photos.

Contents

INTRODUCTION

As I sit here resting on a bench in my back garden on this bright and hot summer's day, surrounded by the beautiful flowers in their stunning array of vibrant colours, I lazily watch as some birds fly into the garden to the feeders that I had provided for them earlier that morning, the starlings squabbling and pecking at each other as they do so. A robin, who had also flown into our garden, hops quite contentedly along, eagerly pecking at the food that the greedy starlings had flicked to the ground.

In a corner near to where I sit, we have a patch of wildflowers to encourage wildlife, their fragrant aromas, including the sweet smell of lavender, fill the air with their strong scent, attracting the butterflies which flutter between the blooms.

The sun is shining brightly and the sky is a clear shade of blue with a few white clouds.

I have my faithful dog Gambit lying contentedly by my side. And I am feeling blissfully happy and very relaxed as a slight welcoming breeze blows softly around us on this hot, humid day.

I allow my mind to wander back to cherished memories of my childhood and of my loving parents, and of the house in which I grew up. I have so often throughout the years thought about my parents and of growing up during the Sixties in a working-class family, when my father worked hard to make ends meet, and my mum worked just as hard to keep the family home running.

My name is Theresa Jean Ayres, and I am the third daughter of my parents, Violet and Albert Ayres. I was the only one out of their eight children to have been born at home. I grew up in a three-bedroomed council house and I come from a very good and honest hardworking family. I can honestly say that I am very proud of it. My parents, who struggled financially throughout my childhood raising us children, always made sure that we were always fed and clothed, that we were always neat and tidy and looking our best. They taught us manners and how to be polite to other people, and most of all, they provided us children with a home that was full of security and love.

Like all childhoods, there were some good times and also some bad times. And if anyone was to ask me, what I would want to change about myself, I would say, without any hesitation, my shyness. You see I have been shy since as long as I can remember, and it caused me nothing but unnecessary suffering throughout my childhood. I was not only just shy, but I was so timid and nervous around people, so much so that it left me with an inability to connect with anybody from outside of my own family. I felt far more happier being in the safety of my home.

Even with members of my own family, such as aunts and uncles, I would be crippled by my inability to speak—as if afraid that by opening my mouth I would draw to much attention to myself.

Being unable to speak up soon made me a target for cruel children at school. I became a victim because

I was too scared, or rather, should I say, afraid to stand up for myself. So, I was faced with nothing but being bullied and suffering intimidation by those who found me to be an easy target, and there was absolutely nothing that I could do to prevent it from happening.

But it wasn't just the children that tormented me, even some adults seemed to take a delight in mocking me, and one particular incident left me completely traumatised.

Back then nobody knew why I suffered so much from my lack of confidence, my fears and my shyness, and it would only be years later as an adult, under the guidance of a professional hypnotherapist, that I would learn the secrets which my mind had locked away out of fear and trauma. But, as a child, I really did have nowhere to turn to, and if it hadn't been for my parents, and of the loving stable home life that they had provided for me and my siblings, I don't know how I would have coped.

This is why I have been compelled to write this book.

To tell the story not just that of my life, but also that of my parents who were always there for us children, no matter what. Of my mother who was left orphaned at the age of just five and who had never known or experienced a stable and loving childhood like the one she gave to me. And my father, who spent the early years of his childhood on the road living in a horse drawn wagon and of his family, and of discovering my Romany roots.

It is about my memories of a childhood that I have often thought about throughout my life, and which I will never forget. Those treasured memories, like the powerful smell of lavender polish whenever I came home from school, or of the delicious smell of a Sunday roast cooking in the oven. Of hot summers and cold winters, of coal fires burning away in the hearth which would only warm up that one particular room, and of freezing cold nights when we would wake up in the mornings with ice on the inside of our windows. My memories of playing games using only our imagination with my two older sisters in our back garden. And the fond memories of our occasional exciting day trip out to the fairground and seaside.

It's the story of a childhood that was filled with laughter and tears, of the good times and the bad. How I grew up learning to face challenges throughout my childhood. Learning what was important in life, learning to have respect for others and of overcoming my fears.

The fun and laughter that we shared between me and my family and of the obstacles and traumas I was forced to face. And also, of the struggles that I had experienced, and of how I learned to cope with whatever life threw at me.

But most importantly of all, I tell this is to honour my parents Violet and Albert who, no matter what life threw at them, and although they struggled financially in bringing up eight children, (five daughters and three sons) they were always there for me and my siblings. Of how my mum's words of wisdom and advice, of a heartfelt plea and of a promise I had made to her — they have remained with me throughout my life, and have never been forgotten.

I was not only a victim. I was a survivor.

This is my story, of a girl called Theresa Jean Ayres growing up in a working-class family in the late Fifties and during the Sixties.

CHAPTER ONE
THE COLD MARCH DAY

I was born in March 1955, a year when Winston Churchill still governed the country and Britain was still recovering from the aftermath of the Second World War, which had ended a decade ago.

I came into the world on a bitterly cold day when snow had been falling throughout the night and which had left a carpet of snow which turned everything white on that very morning. And my dad would tell me on several occasions about how he had had to go out in a blizzard when Mum had gone into labour with me, trundling through the snow to get to a phone box so that he could call the midwife out.

I was born in a council house on Down Street in Molesey. a small town in surrey on the edge of London, about half a mile south of the Thames and a mile west of Hampton Court and Bushy Park. My parents, I believe, were at the time living in shared accommodation with my mother's brother and sister-in-law and their two daughters. I would grow up and spend my childhood in West Molesey in Surrey, which was once a small village that dates back as far as the Doomsday Book. It was then surrounded by green fields, orchards and farmland. There were three old churches including St Peter's, where I was christened; a few schools, a village hospital, a fire station, and an old police station built in about 1900, which was run by the Metropolitan Police.

I can recall Mum telling me that when she first came to Molesey in the 1940s there used to be a large pond near to where we lived. There were still farms and an orchard when I was a child, and can remember running home from school one day, very excited at having seen a farmer with a stick in his hand, walking very briskly with a pig trundling along in front of him.

After I was born the council house became a bit overcrowded, and as they so desperately needed somewhere else to live my dad got in touch with a local councillor who eventually helped my parents to move into new accommodation in Spreighton Road. A home where I was to spend my childhood under the watchful and loving eye of my proud parents.

CHAPTER TWO
MY HOME IN SPREIGHTON ROAD

One of my earliest memories I have of my childhood is of me walking along beside Mum as we strolled beside the river that led into Hampton Court. I know this because the river was on the left-hand side of us.

I was about two or three years old and I was clutching hold of the side of an empty pushchair, and even now I can visualise what that pushchair looked like rather well. It was quite a sturdy heavy pushchair with thick chrome handles. The seat and backrest were cream or whitish in colour, sitting atop a chrome metal base with a footrest that you could pull right out.

I can remember wearing a light jacket or coat, so it must have been early evening or early spring, when we had taken that walk. There were a few people about and Mum had tried to pick me up to put me back into the pushchair so that I would not get tired. But I did not want to go into the pushchair at all, and I rebelled and tightly clutched hold of the pushchair in defiance. Mum gently persuaded me to let go, and eventually she was able to pick me up and gently put me back, and she had then rather hurriedly strapped me in.

We were to, throughout the years; continue our walks into Hampton Court.

*

Despite the years that have passed I can remember our home in Spreighton Road as if I had only visited their just yesterday. It was on a long road with a row of neat brick terraced houses. Each house had a small front garden, boarded with a concrete fence, which divided the house from the neighbour's and from the public path. I can remember the garden being fairly small, with a number of colourful flowers and beautiful scented roses that bloomed around the edge.

The pavement path leading up to the front door had a couple of large, steep steps. I believe they were reddish in colour, and I can remember very often my mum being on her hands and knees polishing the steps until they shone.

Around the right side of the house was a pathway that led up to a very tall wooden gate, which opened through into our back garden. The back garden, from what I can remember – and can picture in my mind – was rather long but not very wide. There was a grassy patch in the middle with some flowers around the verges. I remember the day, years later, when Granddad came over to help Dad build a shed out in the garden. Dad had grown up on Spreighton Road after his family had settled down and, as fate allowed, we were only doors away from the house where my paternal grandparents still resided with some of their other children and their families too.

Inside of our house, my sisters and I had the two back bedrooms while our parents had the one bedroom at the front. Our bedrooms consisted of a bed, a wardrobe and a chest of drawers. I can remember of the games we used to play, especially during the spring or summer months when we should have been in bed but was still light outside. My sisters and I would try to go around the bedroom without touching the floor, using the wardrobe and chest of drawers to clamber on. I can still visualise myself jumping from the bed and onto the windowsill, then sliding along on my behind across to where the chest of drawers was and trying to get from the windowsill to that unit without landing on the floor. It was such great fun as we each tried to beat the other two around the room. But the thumping banging and giggling of our antics would soon become quite noisy and it wasn't long before Mum heard all the commotion and she would call up the stairs for us to get back into our beds, which my sisters and I rather reluctantly would do.

Coming out of our bedroom was the landing where, on one side, there was a small square or oblong window, with a reasonably sized windowsill, which overlooked the side of the house. As a small child I was always fascinated by an ornament which my mum had put on display there. It was of a figurine of a grand lady, on the side of her the porcelain had been made to look like she was near a brick wall. I believe it could have been a sort of vase, although I cannot remember if there were ever flowers in it.

Downstairs there was a fair-sized living room where the window looked out into the front garden, there was a sofa and two armchairs, and a wooden sideboard situated against the wall. There was a nice sized dining table and dining room chairs, which, when I was a child, looked rather grand; I liked the way the whole middle cushioned seat could come completely out. There was a fireplace opposite the window, which had a mantelpiece with a clock standing in the middle. I can recall Mum having her armchair right next to the fireplace, for those winter days when a crackling fire would have been most warming and welcoming. My parents also had a treasured photo, in a lovely frame, of my two older sisters, Jennifer and Pearl, proudly hanging upon our dining room wall.

One of the things that really stick in my mind while growing up in our house was our black and white television set, which had an arial perched on the top. There was a rather large bulky back to the set, which, made it heavy and took up a lot of space. Whenever we wanted to watch a program on our TV, I could guarantee that the picture would go wrong, causing lines across the screen, making it unbearable to watch sometimes. My dad would fiddle about with the aerial trying to get a perfect picture. I can remember the frustration when watching a television programme only for the screen to break up and the sound to hiss. When it went wrong there were lots of moans and groans from us all, and it would often end with Dad in his frustration, banging on the top of the television, until the picture came back on, or if not, we would either switch off or watch the rest of the programme despite the rather fuzzy screen.

At the back of the house was where our kitchen was situated. It was not very big, consisting mainly of a larder, where we stored our milk, flour, butter, eggs, bread and any other foods. We did not then have neither a fridge nor freezer, so most foods such as milk and butter had to be bought from the shops on a daily basis. Neither did we have an immersion heater, so any hot water that was needed was boiled up in the kettle.

11

Unless as in wintertime then we had the coal fire going, this helped to give us the hot water that we needed. I believe this is because there was a boiler in a cupboard in the hall which heated water, using heat from the coal fire. There was a large white and very deep sink, with old fashioned taps and a draining board and a small cooker, and also a cupboard for storing cooking utensils, which had a set of drawers where Mum kept our knives, forks and spoons.

There was, located to one side of the kitchen, by the cooker, a wooden table and chairs where we would all sit to eat. And, by the table, there was our toilet, which lay behind a large wooden panelled door. Back in those days hygiene was not a big factor, and houses that had indoor toilets often had them in the kitchen. The toilet door had an old-fashioned latch that was used to open it. The door was painted, I believe, green or blue, and the toilet cistern had a pull chain to flush. It was most unpleasant when someone needed to go to the toilet while Mum was cooking or if you were eating your food at the table.

A back door led out from the kitchen and out into the back garden. To your right of the door, nearest the gate, was where the dustbin and the small pig bins were stored for food waste, like potato peelings or scraps of cabbage and other vegetable waste, which would be collected and go to the local farm.

Our garden was reasonably long, and at the bottom was a high wooden fence which split the garden from our neighbour's. At the bottom of the fence there was a mound of dirt and grass which sloped up where you could stand and which went from one side to the other. I can remember times when I would step up onto the mound and then gingerly peer over the top of the fence to see if the other children from the house opposite were outside playing in their garden.

I have so many happy and cherished memories of playing, reading and even getting up to mischief in this very garden. I can remember having so much fun playing with my sisters, and of entertaining and keeping myself occupied that, I would on occasions, become so completely engrossed in what I was doing that my mum would have to call me to come in to get ready, as we had to go and pick up my younger sister from school.

They truly are very happy memories indeed.

CHAPTER THREE
FAMILY LIFE

As a child I became increasingly shy, so shy that I found it very hard to communicate with anybody, whether they were adult or child, from outside of the comfort and safety of my home.

At home though, I could just be myself, and like any child I could be naughty on occasion. I had arguments and fights with my sisters, and could, sometimes, be rather disobedient. But I grew up respecting my mum and dad, and never forgot all that they taught me. I never stole from anyone, or took what was not mine. I was never rude to anyone I met or knew, and never answered an adult back or was rude to them. But I wasn't a saint, and could be quite selfish at times. I loved dolls, and had a few, but I would never allow my sisters to ever play with them.

I was a small, timid, shy girl with brown eyes like Mum's, and I had long dark brown hair, which I liked to have plaited and tied with lovely colourful ribbons. My pleasure came in books; full of stories and nursery rhymes, a picture story book of *Little Women*, *Tales of Noddy* and of other Enid Byton stories. I also, as a child, believed in fairies; I had a book that I really liked that had drawings of fairies and pixies. I would often daydream about what it would be like if I was to see a fairy or these small little pixies as portrayed in my book. I can remember once looking around the garden, just to see if I could actually find them.

I don't know why, but I had a fascination with buttons. Mum had a deep round tin which had drawings and coloured markings around it, and it was full of buttons; of all different sizes and colours. Sometimes, whenever I was home from school ill, I would get Mum's tin out and sit at the dining room table, and I would take a handful of buttons out and lay them out in neat rows in front of me. I would sit there for hours, studying each button and then matching them with the different buttons that were on display. I do not know why I had this fascination for playing with Mum's buttons. But I do now, as an adult, have my own tin of buttons.

I loved biscuits, and I soon earned the nickname 'Biscuit Ayres' from my mum, because when I was a toddler, Mum and Dad had found me hiding in the cupboard, quite happily munching away on a packet of chocolate biscuits. And like most children, I had a fondness for sweets, and my favourite chocolate was chocolate buttons.

And then there were my toys. We were not a wealthy family, so my sisters and I were always grateful for whatever Mum and Dad bought for us. My most valued toys were a dog and a teddy bear that I always slept with, which I had named Sooty and Sweep, and a doll which I had named Susy, and which was very fragile. Sooty and Sweep and Sue were at the time very popular children's characters on Television.

A night time was also a concern as, the thing that I hated and feared more than anything was the dark. I can remember on many nights that I would play my mum up after she and Dad had gone to bed, because as I laid there in the dark, I had a terrible fear of something happening to me. I couldn't see anything and often thought I was somewhere else, unfamiliar and away from the safety of my bedroom. So, I would continually call out for the light to be turned on, and in the end and, because I was keeping everyone else awake, Mum would leave the landing light on for me.

CHAPTER FOUR
OUR WAY OF LIFE – GROWING UP IN THE SIXTIES

Life in the Sixties was so very much different from what it is today. Our way of life and how we lived was very much harder, especially if you were from a working-class family everything was done by hand and cooking made from scratch.

It was the custom that it was the woman's place to stay at home; they had the responsibility of looking after the children, doing the housework, cooking the meals, doing the sewing and going down to the local shop to buy that day's groceries. And it was the man's job and duty to go out to work and to provide for his wife and family by working long hours, Monday to Fridays: ensuring that he and his family always had plenty of food on their table.

Every day and early in the mornings, you would hear the jangling of glass bottles as the milkman came down the street in his milk float delivering pints of milk to our house and to those of our neighbours. Fruit, vegetables and meat were all locally sourced.

Life in our home was always very busy and hectic for Mum. After Dad went off to work early in the morning, Mum started busily doing the household chores. The start of a busy day would begin by getting us children ready for school; Mum would prepare our breakfast, which would normally be porridge or cereal. She would then take the youngest children to school – the older children would make their own way on foot – then do the shopping before returning home to start her daily rituals.

I hated Mondays. Poor Mum, even now I can see her with loads of dirty clothes on the kitchen floor, waiting to be washed. We did not have automatic washing machines or tumble dryers in the Fifties and Sixties, machines that are essential for today's day and age. Mum had a machine that could only wash the clothes but didn't rinse them; I can only remember the machines Mum used, but not the makes. The washing machine was a tall, rather slim looking contraction, with a lift-up lid at the top. Mum would put the washing inside the drum, shut the lid and start up the machine.

Unfortunately, the washing would get terribly tangled up and Mum would have to use long wooden tongs to help untangle the items of clothing and then pull out the heavy sopping wet washing. As the machine didn't rinse the water out, you would have to do this by hand, though Mum did this by using a wringer, a metal frame on each side which held two large rollers which you would operate by turning a handle on the side of the frame. Mum would turn the handle with one hand while feeding the washing into the rollers with her other hand. Water used to slosh everywhere, it was very wet and messy work and very slow too.

Afterwards Mum would then have to carry the washing outside into the garden to hang it on the line to dry. During the summer it was not so bad for drying, but during the winter months the clothes sometimes used to freeze. I can still picture Mum even now, as she struggled against the cold, attempting to peg or unpeg washing with hands that were frozen.

Mum must have spent nearly the entire day doing this, week after week, along with all the other chores she had. And the following day Mum would have to stand ironing all the clothes that she had washed the day before.

I can remember three irons that Mum had all different sizes and made of cast iron that you would have to heat up by putting in front of the fire, before you ironed your clothes. Another chore Mum had was washing the kitchen floor on her hands and knees with a scrubbing brush.

Often, once the washing was complete and drying it would be time for Mum to pick up the children from school. Mum always did her best in keeping a clean and tidy house, and I can remember many a time coming home from school and opening the back door to be greeted by the strong pleasant smell of lavender polish. Even now, the smell brings back those memories of home; Mum used to love polishing the living room and would polish it from top to bottom. The table, the sideboard and even the wooden chair frames; the entire house always smelt clean of lavender.

Once all the children were home Mum would prepare the dinner for when Dad came home from work. When Mum cooked roast beef all the fat from the meat would go into a basin and be left to cool down, when it would harden into lard. This was called beef dripping. Looking back now, it was probably not one of the healthiest things to eat, but for us children, it was a delight. My sisters and I would sit at the table and enjoy having our slice of bread and dripping, thoroughly relishing the taste.

Mum worked so hard and tirelessly during the week days, and one of the things that I hated her doing more than anything else was when I would find her perched on a window sill, leaning backwards out of an upstairs window, so that she could reach to clean them. I used to be so terrified that she would fall, and so I would always be so relieved when she had finished and had stepped down from the window.

It wasn't until the evening times, when all of us children were in bed, that Mum would find a couple of hours to sit in front of the television and have a well-earned cup of tea with Dad.

Mum and Dad did not only provide us with a stable and loving household, but also taught us the important aspects of life, educated us with lessons, knowledge and words of wisdom. I was told about the loyalty of family, and to never look down at another person less fortunate than you, and to always try to do my best. And also, if there was one thing that I was taught, it was that you always had respect for the law, and if you were ever approached by a policeman and he asked what you were doing, you always answered them politely. There were a lot of police around then, not just where I lived, but everywhere. They were a part of our community and you never dared be rude or answer them back. After all, they were there to help us. Mum used to tell me that if you ever got lost or needed help always ask a policeman. I knew from an early age that they were there to protect us, and for us to go to whenever we needed help. Although I was unsure if I would ever have had the courage of approaching a policeman if I had needed assistance.

When I was at school, there used to be one policeman that used to pass by the school regularly on his rounds, and a group of children used to poke their heads through the railings waiting for him to go by. He would frequently stop for a chat.

"Are you all being good?" he used to ask, standing there on the pavement outside, dressed smartly in his uniform, with his helmet sat on his head. He was always greeted by the many excited voices all talking at once.

"So, what have you all been learning today?" he would ask. He was very friendly, always chatting and laughing at some of the comments that the children were making, or questions they were asking him. And one day I actually walked up to the railings with the other children and I can remember him looking directly over at me and smiling and saying hello, and I as usual and regrettably I went all shy. I just could not answer him, not even to say a very quick hello.

I loved watching him though as he chatted away to us children, it was something I looked forward to during playtime. To me he was someone very important. He was a policeman and he was there to protect us all, that was his job. I had so wanted to talk and chat with him just like the other children were doing, but unfortunately, I just couldn't I had always been just too shy, to even say anything at all to him. (What a wimp was I.)

*

Sometime during the weekday, maybe once a week, Mum would find the time to sit and have a chat and a cup of tea with her friend whom she had known for years, Betty Woods, a housewife who lived across the road and a few doors down from us with her husband and children. Back in those days you did not need to lock your doors, and neighbours or friends could just simply give a slight tap on the door, poke their head around and let themselves in. Mrs Woods was a regular visitor and Mum enjoyed her company very much.

I can still picture even now, my mum sitting there at the table with Mrs Woods, drinking cups of tea, and having a good gossip and a chat. It was so pleasant seeing Mum looking happy and having a good laugh.

Mum would get her shopping daily, and sometimes I would go down to the shop with her. Moffatts was near the end of our road, and it was run by a friendly husband and wife. On occasion, while she bought some groceries for that day, Mum would allow me to choose some sweets. On a Thursday Mum would give the husband a list of items that she wanted, and he would prepare a box of groceries which she would collect the following day. He did this every week for Mum so that she would have all the food she needed for that weekend.

I think it was only once a week that the Corona van would stop near our house, always during the late afternoons. It was much like an ice cream van, though Corona was originally a Welsh company which produced a variety of fizzy drinks such as Orangeade,

Cherryade, Lemonade, Cream Soda and Limeade, which used to come in tall glass bottles. Sometimes Mum would for a treat buy a bottle or two of this fizzy drink for us. She did not do this often, and once back indoors, she would get some cups out and ask us which we wanted and then pour us all a drink.

Back in those days we had a lot of doorstep deliveries, and apart from the milkman and the Corona van, we also had the coalmen with their clothing always covered in soot, who used to deliver the coal by the sack load. Even the rent was paid for on the doorstep.

Fresh fruit and veg could be bought off a gentleman named Jack who always travelled around in a horse-drawn cart. My sisters and I used to watch from the window as Jack rode away, his horse's hooves clacking loudly on the road, no sooner had he left than we would see some of our neighbours hurrying out from their houses with spades in their hands. They would rush to the spot where Jack had stopped and scoop up the manure left behind by his horse and carry it back to their gardens.

But, one of the most exciting things being a child was when, during the warmer weather, the ice cream vans made their rounds. As with all children in the early evening during the warm or hot weather, whenever I heard the van coming down our road, with its chimes jingling loudly, I would rush to the window to peer out, to see where it had stopped, watching the other children as they made haste towards it. I would then ask Mum if I could have an ice cream and, on the odd occasion, Mum would give me some money to go out to the van to buy one each for us children. But Mum didn't always have the money to spare, so could not always afford to buy us all an ice cream, and Mum and Dad certainly did not like treating one without the others, so Mum quite often and rightly so, had to say no. And although I may have given a little moan, I completely understood why. So, it was always a special treat whenever Mum could give us money for an ice cream.

Mum would give Jenny some money and we would run out to the van quite excited and got ourselves a cornet, which was sprinkled with chocolate strands and sauce. I really enjoyed my ice creams, and because we didn't have them that often, I truly savoured every lick that I took.

Life in our household was always very busy and hectic, and when I wasn't at school, I would occupy myself by playing with my dolls, colouring in books, doing puzzles, or doing my drawings. Another thing that I always liked doing was writing stories, and sometimes drawing the pictures for them as well.

Throughout my childhood, I would sometimes sit on the carpet in the living room in front of the fire, and I would get some of Mum's old stockings and some old bits of sheets and I would make up my very own rag doll. I had a fascination with them, so would on many occasions create my own. They were obviously never perfect, but I always liked the finishing result.

With my sisters in our garden, or if I was at school, there were many fun ways that us children would entertain ourselves. We enjoyed the usual games that were the custom then –hopscotch, skipping, kiss chase or hula hoops – and I loved playing a game of rounders' where you would hit the ball with the bat and run around the bases, hopefully before the other team could get you out. All these games were very popular when I was a child, and I had great fun playing with my sisters, sometimes creating our own games.

For some, what we had may not have seemed all that much, but for us it was everything that we ever needed and wanted.

And looking back now, to me at the time growing up in the Sixties, it was just perfect.

CHAPTER FIVE
A TYPICAL WEEKEND AND A SUNDAY ROAST

I can remember the weekends spent at home so well when I was a child, and sitting here now writing this, the memories are so clear that it's just like I have been transported back to the past.

I can still smell the aroma of a delicious roast lamb dinner, cooking in the oven. The sound of Mum and Dad discussing everyday topics as Mum busied herself preparing the vegetables, peeling the potatoes for roasting. The smells in the living room of lavender polish which always lingered in the air. The sound of the wireless blares out the songs of that era, and often of us children squabbling amongst ourselves as we kept ourselves amused or occupied.

Happy sounds from a happy memory.

During the winter there would be the smell and warmth of a coal fire, where the flames flickered, and the dense smoke would go billowing up through the chimney flue and out through the chimney tops.

The winters truly were the worse time, as the days were often harsh and bitter, and with no central heating, the only source of warmth came from the fire or the kitchen when Mum was cooking. Whenever it was bitterly cold the windows in our bedroom were icy, the glass hazy on both sides with frost; the rooms chilly and the floor always cold under our bare feet.

Every morning I would, after having washed, hurry downstairs and get myself dressed in front of the fire. It was something that my sisters and I would often do, even as teenagers and had left school; we would still change in front of the warmth of the glowing fire. My dad never really approved, and he used to scold and moan at us when we did this.

"You shouldn't be changing in front of us," he would say. "It is not right!"

"It's ok Dad, I am your daughter," I would laugh, hurriedly slipping my shirt over my head as my sisters and I huddled around the crackling fire. Though all in all Dad never really took any notice of us; he used to just walk out of the room when he realized that we were going to continue dressing in front of the fire, whether he liked it or not. In some ways I felt slightly sorry for my dad, the things he used to have to put up with, with five of us daughters.

Every Saturday Mum would be busy as usual, either tidying the breakfast cutlery ready for washing or tending to my younger siblings. Dad would be sitting at the kitchen table with the newspaper, checking out which horses were running and of which he should place a bet on.

For us children Saturday mornings were really determined by the weather. If the day was cold or rainy, we would remain inside and occupy ourselves with our own games or other activities that would keep us entertained for the morning. But if the day was not too bad then Mum would allow me and my two older sisters to take a walk down the road to look around the shops. This was something that I enjoyed doing with my sisters, and Mum would give each of us some money to spend on ourselves, and sometimes, if there was anything that she needed at the shops, Mum would give Jenny some extra money so that she could collect it for her. I would then kiss Mum goodbye, and she - as always – would tell us to be careful and to mind the road. (This is something that I even now tell my own children and grandchildren whenever they too go out.) So, off we would go, quite excited to be going out on our own without a grown up accompanying us.

As our granddad lived up the road from us, and we would have to pass their house, we would often pop in to say hello, especially to our aunt Edith. She would always enquire after Mum and ask if she was well, and before leaving, we would always ask if there was anything that they would like us to get for them at the shops. Most times they never did, but other times it would be just something small, and most of the time, as we got ready to go, my aunt would give each of us a threepence or sixpence to spend. We would always politely decline the offer, just as Mum had always taught us to do, but our aunt was persistent, so Mum would have been ok with us taking it. as she would often tell us, "If the person really wants you to really have the money, they will still give it to you anyway."

So, we would go to East Molesey to Woolworths or another shop. As always on a Saturday, it was busy with children and other families out. My parents, especially Mum, would always warn us about talking to strangers; this was one of the most important things that she taught us.

Mum would often say, "You are not to speak to anyone you do not know; you do not take sweets or anything from them, you don't talk to them and, most importantly of all, you do not go off with them."

"Yes, Mum, we'll be careful," my sisters and I would always reply. It was an important life lesson, but as much as we listened to our parents, and with me being so shy and unable to hold conversations with other people, I didn't think anything like that would ever happen to me. But, as I found out on one shopping trip, the most unexpected can happen, and that throws you completely off your guard and takes you by surprise.

It was on one of our usual Saturday morning shopping trips when the unexpected was to happen. My sisters and I had set out early, visited our aunt and uncle, and had walked to East Molesey and we were happily browsing the items in the shops and pondering what we could buy with the sixpences we had been given.

I remember us going into Woolworths and gazing at the variety of sweets and chocolates and deciding what we were each going to buy. I purchased my usual bag of chocolate buttons, and after paying for our goods, and clutching our bags tightly, we exited the shop, and started the slow walk home.

We chatted happily together as we walked along the busy pavement, excitedly talking amongst ourselves, eager to get home so that we could show Mum what we had bought, exchanging comments and happily discussing about what we were going to be doing for the rest of the day. Often, we would walk single file and I would often be last in line, deep in my own thoughts or daydreaming, a thing I often did during my childhood. And that day, as we made our way home, I was so absorbed with my thoughts and feeling quite happy with myself that I was oblivious to what was going on around me, when suddenly I was bought back to reality with a jolt.

A hand suddenly reached down and grabbed my arm tightly and I turned, startled, and looked up to see a strange bloke, who I had never seen before in my life, standing beside me, his face expressionless. My heart froze in my chest, my breath caught in my throat, and I tried frantically to pull my hand away, but he held me firm, turning my arm around and prying my fingers open with his other hand.

Jenny and Pearl both spun around, faces shocked. Before anyone could react, he shoved something into my hand before he quickly hurried off. I can tell you it quite put the wind up me; I glanced down to see what he had put into my hand and saw that it was a Polo mint. Now, I don't know if Jenny thought I was going to pop it into my mouth, but she moved quick and slapped the Polo out of my hand.

"Don't eat it Theresa, it could be poisoned," Jenny warned.

"I wasn't going to eat it!" I told her.

I remembered what Mum had always told us and I was quite shocked. I was definitely not going to eat that mint. The three of us headed for home and we decided it was best not to tell Mum about the incident.

*

It was the Saturday afternoons that I dreaded the most; it was the same every weekend throughout my childhood. Dad would come home from the pub, have his dinner while we either played or sat idly at the table watching as Dad ate his food and listening to the comments and discussions that passed between him and Mum. Then, afterwards, Dad would go into the living room and switch on the television to watch the horse racing.

Now, this was the time of day I actually hated, because that's when Dad used to like us to remain quiet and, if we did make a noise, he would moan and tell us off. Dad loved watching the horse racing and it was a firm rule that he had to have silence so that he could watch and listen to the results.

I can remember that on many occasions I went outside to avoid any confrontation with Dad. It was not because he was an unkind person; he was just so desperate for a win, to see his horse cross the finishing line ahead of the other horses.

And again, after tea, Dad would listen to the score draw of the football, which both he and Mum used to do. Dad would sit there crossing off the teams as the chap on the telly called out the selected teams. I didn't understand or know much about football or of how it worked, so it was a thing that never interested me. I only know that throughout their lives they continued doing the football pools in the hope that one day their luck would come and all their dreams would come true, but sadly it never did, and they never got the chance of celebrating a big win. I am rather sad about that, because if there were two people deserving of having their lives changed and being able to live comfortably, then it was my mum and Dad.

CHAPTER SIX
SUNDAY EVENING SING-A-LONG
BY THE WIRELESS.

On Sundays it could be rather busy and certainly hectic for Mum. Whilst the roast dinner was cooking in the oven, which was mainly a delicious roast lamb, which we would always eat with some mint, and while the potatoes were roasting nicely in the lamb's fat, I would kiss my mum good morning, and have a drink and some toast, before wandering out into the back garden to play.

Mum would come to the door and call us all in one at a time for our hair to be washed. I hated having my hair washed and I always knew precisely when it was time for it, as Mum always had the wireless on listening to the Billy Cotton Show featuring a man who would always bellow out in a very loud voice, "Wakey! Wakey!"

"Theresa!"

In turn we each were called and in we would go.

I hated it!

Up on the stool and leaning over the kitchen sink as Mum poured jugs of water over my head, I would squirm and wiggle and protest, keeping my eyes tightly closed.

"Theresa! Will you stand still?"

And then afterwards to have my hair brushed and combed; I had long hair and it would sometimes become tangled. Mum was never rough when she brushed our hair but I still dreaded it.

One day I got very rebellious and when Mum called out for me to come on inside, I ran down the garden. I don't know why I did, perhaps I thought that I would get out of having my hair washed and I would be able to continue playing in the garden, and that would be that.

But no.

Mum came marching down the garden after me, and when she caught me, she was not amused at all, and I was given a good talking too. Not just about my being defiant to her, but also because I had, after all, made her have to come after me, which to be fair, she didn't have the time to do. So, Mum took me indoors and I had to endure having my hair washed.

In the afternoons when Dad came home from the pub and after he had eaten his dinner, he would sit in the armchair and, most times, he would eventually have a snooze.

When he did, my sisters and I would get some of my ribbons and we would start tying them into his hair. When we had finished, we would laugh and giggle at how ridiculous we had made Dad look with his hair covered in coloured bows and ribbons. Mum used to shake her head, smiling at the antics we were getting up too and, poor Dad, when he woke up wondered what on earth was on his head, and when he realized what we had done to him he started pulling them out and it sent us all into fits of giggles. Dad, as always, just took everything all in his stride.

Sometimes, when Dad came home from the pub, he would bring a small bottle of light brown ale and a bottle of lemonade home with him. And, after he had finished his dinner, he would get a large jug or bowl and then he would pour the beer and the lemonade in together and mixed it up, sloshing it together to make a frothy bowl of Shandy. He would then let each of us have just a small mouthful to taste.

Although Dad made sure that the Shandy was weak and had more lemonade than ale, I did not care for it very much. I disliked the bitter taste and I don't remember if I ever tried it more than once. Other times, he would give us each a sixpence, and my sisters and I would all go out to the small little off-license where we could buy ourselves some treats.

My dad would perform a trick which Mum strongly disapproved of, and whenever he used to perform this trick in front of us, Mum would tell him off. But he didn't take any notice, especially when my sisters and I would crowd around where he sat and encouraged him to show us again and again. Dad would perform this trick quite a few times before Mum lectured him so much that eventually he had to stop.

"You shouldn't be showing them things like that!" Mum would tell him. And, looking back now, I can see from Mum's point of view for it was quite dangerous. But, being a child, I did not see the danger, only the magical hold the trick had, and I was enthralled by what Dad did.

"Please Dad, show us again," we would all plead. Dad smiled and picked up his box of matches from the armrest from where he sat, and we all cheered excitedly for what was to come.

He used to get out a match and, with a single swipe, light it up and hold it up in his hand until the flame took hold. With our wide eyes we stared at this small dancing flame in delight, the smell of the sulphur stinging our nostrils as we watched with excitement. Then Dad put the lighted match into his open mouth and closed his mouth over the lit flame. He then took the now extinguished match with its blackened head out of his mouth and held it for us to see.

We all thought it was great, and I would ask him how he did it, why hadn't it burnt his mouth. I thought he was very clever, although now I can see why Mum hated Dad showing us that trick and can completely understand why she got upset with him, whenever he did show us.

In the evenings after tea, it was time for us to relax. We would all sit down around the television and watch Pinkie *and Perky*, the two puppet pigs that used to sing and dance. And then, afterwards it would be time for each of us children to have a strip-wash or a bath in front of the fire.

Mum would use an old tin bath that she and Dad had, place the bath in front of the fire and fill it up using a jug, and then, one at a time, my sisters and I in turn would be washed, dried and then dressed into our nighties and made ready for bed. But, before we retired for bed, there was a very special time we spent with Dad. He would sit himself down in his chair every Sunday evening and my other sisters and I, all now washed, would all sit on the floor around him, or up on his lap, and he would sing songs to us. The most famous one that I can remember, and which has always remained in my mind, and which I as a young child enjoyed immensely was 'I've Got Sixpence to Spend':

I've got sixpence, Jolly. Jolly, sixpence,
I've got sixpence to last me all my day
I have tuppence to lend
And tuppence to spend
And tuppence to take home to
My wife.

Sometimes whilst singing to us he could be quite serious, while other times he might be humorous and playful. Like the time he took my favourite teddy bear, Sooty, and placed it on his foot, and as he sang my favourite song to me, he flipped his leg so that my teddy went sailing through the air and landed on the floor on the opposite side of the room.

I would squeal and go running after my bear and Dad would laugh, and probably do it for a second time before I would then, rather wisely, keep my Sooty tucked safely under my arm and away from him. But it was such fun, and we would be, before going to bed, Mum, Dad, my sisters and I, sitting together, singing along to the songs being played on the wireless. One song in particular that still sticks in my mind was 'Run Rabbit Run'.

It was such great fun.

These are the songs that I mostly remember my dad singing to me on those very special Sunday evenings. Old songs he sang with a charm which filled me with warmth I still feel today; when I remember back to those treasured times of a childhood I shall never forget:

Church on Time', 'Ride a cock horse to Banbury Cross', 'It's a Long Way to Tipperary', 'Bye Bye Black Bird', 'Horsey, Horsey (Don't You Stop)', 'Daisy, Daisy (Give Me Your Answer Do)'.

This is what I shall always remember the most about my past and, even now, these memories hold a special place in my heart.

CHAPTER SEVEN
WHISKY & RUM

Sometimes, as in any family, something can suddenly happen that will take you completely by surprise and disrupt your pleasantly calm, organised and routine home.

And my family was no exception. Because in my family too it could be utter chaos, where anything could suddenly happen, that could turn our home into sudden turmoil.

It happened on a normal Sunday afternoon, and I can recall that afternoon very well.

We had finished having our dinner of roast beef or lamb, which Mum always cooked to perfection, served with her homemade roast potatoes and Yorkshire puddings and green cabbage.

Mum always did us a pudding which was either plums or prunes with custard, which, apparently, was very good for the digestive system.

After we had all finished eating Mum would clear away the plates and cutlery and wipe the table down, and she would then do the washing up while my sisters and I played with our toys in the living room. Mum had already put Dad's dinner into the oven to keep warm for him for when he came home. Then as we usually did on a Sunday afternoon, we waited for Dad to come home from the pub.

And I can remember that particular afternoon so very well. On hearing Dad coming in through the back door, my sisters and I ran into the kitchen, with the youngest toddling along behind, to greet him as we always did.

He stood there at the kitchen door, and I watched as he bent down, and carefully put two adorable tiny kittens onto the kitchen floor.

One was black and white and the other was a brown tortoiseshell. Both were wide-eyed and pointy eared.

"A gift for you all," Dad smiled.

These two little balls of fluff were very unsteady on their feet, and, for a second, I stared in disbelief. I just could not believe my eyes as I watched as they started to become inquisitive and to move very quickly around the kitchen floor, little meows escaping as they explored their new, to them vast, surroundings.

And that was when, to our surprise, all hell broke loose.

My sister Pearl suddenly screeched loudly in absolute fear at these to very cute little kittens that were tottering around our kitchen floor. She ran into the living room and very quickly slammed the door shut behind her and refused to come out until she considered it was safe to do so.

I stood staring after her in surprise. Now why she did that I will never know — I mean it's not like they were Rottweiler's, was it?

And as for Mum? She was just as surprised as we were, but not very happy with Dad. And as he sat himself down at the table to eat his dinner, Mum, in her exasperation, now having two kittens to feed and look after, wanted to know as to why he had brought two kittens' home with him instead of the one that she had agreed too.

Dad explained to her that he had not wanted to leave the one remaining kitten alone, so had decided to bring the two of them home together instead.

And while all this was going on, my sisters and I were on the kitchen floor, screeching and cooing loudly, making a fuss of our new kittens who had started to purr and arch their small backs as our hands gently stroked and cuddled these bundles of joys.

I was absolutely ecstatic; I had never seen kittens before and I absolutely fell in love with them. They were the first pets that I had ever had, and while we girls were all screeching and the noise must have been quite deafening in our house, especially for a usually quiet Sunday afternoon, I was in my absolute glory.

There was a lot of noise and activity going on everywhere. It was absolutely pure pandemonium, with screaming and shouting; in our excitement all of us children were all trying to talk at once.

It took Pearl a little while before she plucked up the courage to finally come out of the living room, being very cautious as she did so.

Mum warned us that if we didn't quieten down, we would frighten the kittens, so when we were finally calm Mum smiled and gave our two kittens a saucer of milk, which they lapped up, making little purring noises as they did so. I must say I was in my element with these two adorable little kittens.

I am unsure of who suggested the names for them, but it was an obvious choice and one that we all agreed on; as Dad liked going for a drink and had bought our two little additions to our family straight from the pub, it was decided to name our kittens Whiskey and Rum.

Our cats remained a part of our family for quite a few years, and one of them developed quite a bond with my mum. Whenever she took my younger sister or brother to infant school it would always walk along behind, following her all the way to school, and would then wait in the playground beside the pram while Mum took my sister into the classroom. Mum would then, before making the journey back home, pick up the cat and put it on the bottom of the pram, giving it a ride home. This happened on many an occasion, and for many years, and was a very spectacular sight to see.

CHAPTER EIGHT
DAD

If there was anyone that could be devoted to their family, then it was my dad.

Albert Ayres, who stood at 5ft 3 tall, was the life and soul of the party. If we attended a wedding, celebration, or even just the occasional family get together, he would always have a great time.

He was a very well-respected man who was liked by those who knew him, and my dad knew many people around Molesey. He was devoted to Mum, and he was a good, honest, hardworking man who was dedicated to his family, and loved nothing more than coming home to us at the end of the working day.

Mum may have been the heart of the family, but Dad was the provider, and like most men of those times he worked hard to provide us with our upkeep. He spent his days working as a labourer, getting to his job by cycling and often working long hours.

Saturday's afternoons he would spend at The Lord Hotham, the local pub, before returning home to watch the horses with a betting slip in his hand. We would have already eaten earlier so Mum would have put his dinner in the oven to keep warm for him until he came home. Afterwards he would, sit and watch the racing, desperately hoping for a win on the horses

But that did not make him a distant father. My dad enjoyed a pint, especially on the Friday nights and was known to quite a few of the local landlords, where he often drank with those who worked with him or knew him well, including friends such as the local vicar, the Rev. John Yeaned. It seemed as if most of Molesey village knew my dad and regarded him highly.

My memories of such a great man are still rich; his traits and ways of life, stories and songs which made him so unique to me. How he would put brylcream in his hair every morning and would come out of the bathroom smelling of the stuff; it always seemed to make his hair look wet and greasy. The way he loved, on the rare occasions that we had them, drenching vinegar on his chip dinners; the sharp tangy smell of it hung in the air — he also had a fondness for pickled onions and gherkins. And, when he had stews, he would love soaking a slice of bread into the leftover gravy.

He enjoyed listening to music and classed The Seekers and Cathy Kirby as firm favourites and enjoyed songs such as 'Scarlett Ribbons (For Her Hair)' and 'Secret Love'.

I fondly remember Dad telling me stories about his childhood and past before settling down with a family. Being so young, my sisters and I would disbelieve when Dad told us about our Romany roots. But Dad felt no shame in his past, only pride, and now I feel this is the reason the Ayres family were always so close.

Albert Ayres was born on Monday 7th December 1925. He was the fourth out of nine siblings and second son to Joseph and Dorothy Ayres, who were, at the time, camped up at Broad Lane Farm, in Walton-on-

Thames in Surrey. Dad spent the first few years of his life travelling the Surrey roads with his family. They worked on the farms for their keep, but still enjoyed the freedom of traveling around the countryside and the country lanes. Then, when my grandparents decided it best to settle down, they were given one of the new houses in Spreighton Road in West Molesey, an area they knew reasonably well.

As Romany travellers who had only known the ways of the free roads and lands, at first my grandparents found adjusting to their new, settled life, quite difficult. They all lived together, sharing the small rooms of the council house, the family expanding with the birth of Dad's siblings who followed; though they were used to tight dwellings from their life out on the roads.

They got on well with their neighbours and they slowly made their house their home, raising their children and remaining in that house on Spreighton Road for the rest of their lives. My dad and his siblings must have had a good childhood and my dad was as close to his older sister, Alice, as he was to his older brother, Joe. Alice mothered her brother, and Dad once said that, as a baby, he was so small that he could sit in a saucer. He was rather late in attending school, much later than other children of his age, so he never really learned to read and write. This was not common among travellers and, maybe, Dad did not take to schooling, but he did struggle with his reading and writing throughout adulthood.

I can remember one occasion from my childhood when I had been sitting having a quite chat with my dad who often entertained me with the adventures he'd had; and he told me of one instance that had occurred when he was a very young man and serving in the army during the war. He was approached by his commanding officer, who had noticed that Dad neither sent or received any letters from home like the other men in the barracks, and wanted to enquire as to why. Dad was quite honest with his commanding officer, explaining that he found it hard to read and write; that was why he could not write home to let his Mum know that he was ok, although he wished that he could do so. The commanding officer was rather alarmed on hearing this, but he was also very sympathetic.

"Well, we can't have that, then," he told Dad. And this commanding officer sat down with Dad and helped him to write a letter, so that he could post it home to his Mum.

My dad would tell me tales of what he got up to as a young man, once the war had ended and he was back in Molesey with his family. He told me that most evenings he and Joe used to go out for a drink at their local pub, The Lord Hotham being known for welcoming the custom of the settled travellers. And Dad and Joe would often meet up with some of the other travellers and they would start the evening warmly with good greetings, laughter and a drink. And, always the night would end spilling out of the pub and onto Walton Road in a brawl of fists and punches. Fist fights between Romany families were common and happened often at The Lord Hotham, but they always end with a handshake and the combatants staggering away for home, only to go through the same routine all over again the following evening.

It was quite hard for me to imagine my dad, who was such small man, having fist fights and brawls in his local pub, and I would like to stress that he was not a bad person. It was just the way they were back then, growing up in the shadows of the war and finding their way into the free world; they liked a drink, but were never aggressively violent, no matter how much they had drunk. They never used weapons either and the fights were always clean. Dad never got into trouble with the police, and most of the time the group of brawling travellers were pulled apart and sent on their way. In fact, my dad knew the local officers quiet well; I can quiet clearly remember a time when my dad went to the pub and helped out a senior police officer with a problem.

A senior police officer whom my dad knew very well had an engagement to attend and my dad had volunteered to look after his police dog for him for the afternoon. My poor Mum was terrified of big dogs, so it was no wonder she was very concerned and apprehensive when this officer turned up with his police dog later that day. Mum spent the whole afternoon trying to keep us away from it, just in case it went for any of us. But there was no problem at all, and I thought it was great.

My dad always liked a drink and, as my mum got to find out throughout their married life, Dad would never change his ways. He often got up to antics and used to bring home stuff like books or crisps. He often returned home, having had a few pints, but he was never violent or abusive to us or to Mum — to him we were his world. In fact, I can never remember my dad ever raising his hand to Mum, he never believed that any man should hit or become aggressive to any woman. And it was my dad, years earlier when he and Mum had first married, who grabbed hold of Mum's brother, Thomas, by the scruff of his neck and literally threw him down the stairs and out of the house the day he saw him lift up his hand to strike Mum during a family dispute.

Dad was loyal to Mum and had been from that very first moment he had seen her. It was true from when they met, a story I had been told many times, but was always just as magical as the first time I had heard it. Violet, who had moved down to Molesey from Weymouth to live with her brother and his family, had been out one evening and, Albert, who had just come out from having had a drink at his local and was quite drunk at the time, fell over a bush right in front of her. And he looked up at her and – I will always remember what he told me – and he said that when he first saw Mum, he told her that she was the woman who he wanted to marry.

Albert and Violet Married, saying their vows at Northern Surrey Register Office on 7th July 1950. They eventually moved into a council house at Down Street in West Molesey, which was close to Spreighton Road, and steadily grew a family, in time having the eight of us children — five daughters, and then three sons.

Before their wedding there had been a rift between Dad and his family, and a lot of the family were not present at Mum and Dad's wedding, but the rift was soon healed. When Albert's sister, Alice, fell very sick and died Dad was very upset; he had such a strong bond with Alice, who had married and moved away from Molesey many years earlier. Dad accompanied his father and Joe and his sisters, making the long journey to Burton-upon-Trent for her funeral.

When I was very young, I never got to see much of Dad, not during the weekdays anyway, because he worked long hours and was often up and gone by the time we all woke up, and we would be in bed again asleep by the time he got home. So, we mainly only saw him at the weekends. Dad always did come home during his lunch break to see Mum; but unless we were off school ill or on our holidays, we wouldn't see him then either.

I do though recall one occasion when I was home sick and Dad did something for me which I will never forget. I had been home from school and I was feeling quite unwell, and being so young and wanting the comfort of my mother instead of the lonesome cold bed upstairs, Mum had made a bed up for me on the sofa so that she could keep a close eye on me, giving me loads of love and attention, making me feel well and safe. Being a housewife, Mum could not sit with me for long, not when she was always so busy, but she often checked on me as I lay dozing.

My sisters and I never had many sweets as Mum and Dad couldn't afford them often. But we did on the odd occasions get treated to some when Mum would take us down to our local shop, which was just up the road to us. We each could select a small box of sweets from the varieties they sold, and I would often choose some marshmallows that were half-coated in chocolate — they were quite delicious. But you couldn't always get them, so I only had them, I believe, on a couple of occasions.

But, on that day when I was laying ill snuggled up in my made-up bed on the sofa, I remember waking up as my dad came in from work to have lunch with Mum. He walked over to where I lay and asked me if I was alright. He then placed a box in my hand and said they were for me for when I was feeling better, and then he left me and walked into the kitchen to have his lunch. When he had gone into the kitchen, I turned the box over in my hand to have a look at what he had bought me, and I couldn't believe my eyes! They were the marshmallows that I had been wanting. Oh, how I held on to them. I was so touched by Dad getting them for me, and for him thinking about me while I was so ill.

I have never forgotten that kind gesture my dad made, and that special memory I have of that moment will remain in my heart forever.

CHAPTER NINE
MY TRIP WITH MUM TO THE HOSPITAL

The earliest memories that I can recall of ever having been away from home and of having been parted from my parents are from when I was about three years old. I had been admitted into hospital to have an operation performed on my eye, a minor procedure, but one which resulted in a lengthy stay in the hospital.

I have to confess that I had found this to be a very unpleasant and traumatic experience. It was not just the fact that I had been left in unfamiliar surroundings, which can obviously be very daunting for any child of that age, or because of the sheer feelings of isolation that I felt being there, but because it was of what I had actually experienced during my stay in the hospital.

It was an experience that had left me feeling very confused and frightened, and which has affected me for the rest of my life, a nightmare will never go away, even today.

I can quite vividly remember holding on tightly to Mum's hand as we waited for our bus (I believe they were trolley buses back then), which would take us to the hospital, where I would have various tests done on my eyes. I can remember being happy, I didn't know where I was going and I really didn't care, I was going out on a trip with Mum and I was very happy, that's all that mattered.

When the bus drew up, Mum helped me on and we sat ourselves down on one of the long seats at the side, near to where the passengers got on and off. There was also a seat facing us which was, at first, unoccupied.

As the bus pulled out and rumbled away, I remember feeling quite excited being there sitting upon Mum's knee, staring out of the window at the passing buildings. To stop me becoming bored, Mum would explain to me and point out various things and objects of interest to help pass the time.

At one of the stops a few people got on and a man sat himself down on the seat adjacent to us. Looking back now upon that day I can remember him having quite a charming nature, and he was very polite and very friendly towards Mum and I. He and Mum exchanged pleasantries with each other, talking about the weather and every day idle chit chat.

He smiled at Mum as he spoke to her, and I turned to look at Mum who smiled back at him as they continued their small conversation. I thought of how radiant she often looked when she smiled, and I can remember him looking over at me and he enquired if I was alright, saying how quiet I was. Mum replied that I was a bit shy, and that I was going to the eye hospital to have some tests. He nodded in acknowledgement, then he looked at me and with a smile and a wink, he proceeded to beckon me to come over and to sit on his lap, tapping his knees with his hands as he did so.

Well, I just didn't know what to do. And as he continually tried to gently coax me to go over and sit on his knee, I suddenly became more shy, and I quickly tuned my face away, burying it in Mum's lap, I didn't know what else to do, and snuggled up into the safety and security of Mum's arms, and as I did so I could hear Mum and the chap laughing humorously.

A short while later we arrived at our destination, and as Mum helped me off of the bus, the chap said goodbye to us and gave me a cheery smile and a wave. I looked back at him and gave him a quick wave back, I then held onto Mum's hand as we set off for the hospital.

I don't remember all that much of walking to the hospital, or entering the strange, vast building with its varnished floors and high walls and that distinguished disinfectant smell. But I do remember the examination and tests.

We were called into an office where a doctor sat behind a large, tidy looking desk and we were invited to sit down. I was seated on a chair while Mum answered a few questions. The doctor folded his hands together, nodded, then turned towards me and asked me some questions. I answered as truthfully as I could, and then I was taken into a different room and seated on a chair at a square table, where a doctor in a white coat proceeded to show me different cards which had certain coloured patterns imprinted in them.

"Now Theresa, what colour is on the card?"

He held each one up right in front of me, coloured blotches and shapes on everyone one.

I looked closely at it.

"It's blue," I answered him.

"And what picture can you see hidden in the card?"

I looked closely at the card again and I thought, 'Wow this is easy. I can go home soon,' and I gave him my honest answer.

The doctor waited anxiously for me to answer as he held up his cards in turn.

"And This one?"

"It's a fish," I said to him, "a green fish."

Afterwards, once the test with the cards were complete, the doctor led me out into the corridor and told me to sit and wait and went back into his office to talk to Mum and report his findings and diagnosis. I can remember sitting on my chair swinging my legs back and forth as I patiently waited for Mum to finish her conversation with the doctor so that we could go home.

It is funny how our mind can deceive us; how you can only recollect certain thoughts of what happened in the past. My mind has no knowledge – is a complete blank – from the moments following when I had my eyes examined to being sat in a hospital bed. It is all a complete mystery. I have no recollection of leaving the eye hospital that day and going home; of saying good bye to my dad, or even if he had accompanied Mum and myself to the hospital when I was admitted — which I doubt, as he had work and would have been unable to have got the time off.

I can't remember having said goodbye to my two sisters or of leaving the house and arriving at the hospital again. And I can't even remember if it was Mum, or the nurses, that undressed me and put me into my nightie and placed me in a hospital bed, where I can only vaguely remember sitting and being terribly upset when Mum left me to go home, leaving me all alone in a strange place with people around me that I didn't know. I cannot even tell you how long my stay was, or of my discomfort after my operation.

The children's ward that I was staying in seemed, to me, very large. There were a number of beds lined neatly along both sides of the walls positioned across from each other. Each bed was immaculate, neat and tidy, and beside each one was a small cupboard with a shelf and a door. The ward itself was immensely clean and bright, with all of the walls painted white, and I will never forget that very strong hospital smell of bleach and disinfectant. Huge double doors were the only way in and out of the ward.

Even being so young, I can remember there was a very strict regime while I was a patient on the children's ward. Hospitals back in those days ran like clockwork and the matrons managed the wards unbendingly everything had to be kept clean and everyone had their place.

Every morning bright and early there would be the hustle and buzzle of activity as the doctors or surgeons did their rounds. They went from bed to bed, talking, questioning and examining their young patients, accompanied by either the ward sister or matron who would have made sure that she had first inspected the wards and seen that everything was in order beforehand. The nurses themselves would hurry on ahead, making sure that I and the other children on the ward were washed and fed. Once the doctors had finished their rounds you would throughout the rest of the day be seen and cared for by the nurse who was on duty.

There was a strict rule in the hospital that one did not get out of bed – you had to remain in bed all day – and I found being in hospital, and away from my mum and Dad, who I missed terribly, was very frightening and a lonely experience. The children's ward was quiet with not much activity or enjoyment, as talking to each other had to be kept to a minimum.

I would anxiously wait for visiting time to come so I would get to see my mum and Dad, who would both visit me every day while I was there. And although I very much enjoyed their visits and the comfort and love they bought each time, I would get very upset and confused when visiting time was over and they went home without me. My young heart ached every time and I was burdened deeply with loneliness at being absent from my family.

I can remember on one occasion when they visited that they surprised me by giving me a doll which my sisters had brought especially for me. I really treasured that doll and I kept it by my side throughout my stay in hospital.

There were two nurses that cared for me throughout my stay in hospital and, every morning, whichever one of them was on duty that particular day, they would come onto the ward and give me a bath, and then put me into a clean nightie, and seen that I was fed, comfortable and ready for the morning visit by the doctor doing his rounds.

Now I sometimes dreaded which nurse I would be seeing each day. One of the nurses I really liked; she was very kind to me, and she was softly spoken and always made me feel at ease. She would always be smiling as she walked onto the ward and asked me if I was ok. Her manner was very pleasant and I loved it when I knew it was her who was on duty for the rest of that day. But the other nurse was the opposite, and when I used to see her coming in through those double doors to start her shift it filled me with dread. Looking back now, she never did anything to hurt me, but I was scared of her as her manner and attitude was completely different to that of the other nurse. She was very harsh and strict; she offered no smiles, no words of comfort, in fact I cannot remember her ever smiling at me or of her being in any way pleasant whilst asking me if I was alright.

As I was so young a child who was deeply missing her family and just wanted to go home and be out of that strange place, it could be rather daunting; she made the ward feel a distressing and lonely place indeed. So, every morning, when I woke up, I would silently be thinking and desperately hoping that it would be the nice nurse who would be on duty that day.

All this makes me wonder if it was the nurse who I dreaded that was on duty on the day of the incident with the grape.

CHAPTER TEN
THE BOY WITH THE GRAPES

I cannot quite remember now of how many children there were on the ward – but I can vaguely remember there being a child of similar age to me who was a few beds down from where I was, but I have no recollection of what he or she looked like.

But I have often thought many times of the boy who occupied a bed across from my own and two beds down. He was slightly older than I was, slim built and very mischievous-looking, often sitting there in bed seemingly without a care in the world.

And there was one day on the ward that I think he must have regretted. It was the day that he was rather generous to me, and I unfortunately caused him quite a stir, and a bit of bother.

It had all begun after we had the usual early morning rounds; I had previously been bathed or washed, had my breakfast and been seen to by the nurse who was on duty that particular day. The matron had done her checks and was satisfied that everything was clean, tidy and spotless; and the doctor had done his rounds, examining the children in care. It is very hard for me to remember what was said to me, but he asked me questions, made a brief examination of my eyes, jotted some notes and left.

There were hushed voices and the clicking of heels as his team walked down the ward and out through those huge doors, and then, very suddenly, there was complete silence — a silence I would never get used to. I sat back against my pillow and glanced around the ward where there wasn't an adult in sight. And still us children remained still and quiet in a fear of breaking the strict rules.

Nobody seemed to move until the boy almost opposite me quickly sat bolt upright and looked around suspiciously, his eyes scanning the ward. I watched intently, curious, knowing that this boy was up to something. I watched as he leant down over the side of his bed and peered into his cupboard, where he rummaged around, the rattling of a brown paper bag seemingly too loud in the stillness of the ward, and then when he sat back up, I saw to my amazement that he had retrieved a bunch of grapes. Although eating was forbidden at that very time the boy casually sat back upon his pillow and pulled one of the grapes free and quickly popped it into his mouth; he looked so relaxed and full of confidence as he chewed happily at his grape.

Wow! I was in awe of this boy, and I was rather envious of him. I knew that we were not supposed to eat anything so early in the morning, and I just could not take my eyes away him sitting up in bed eating grapes without a care.

Defiantly, he plucked another grape from the bunch and threw it into his mouth. I thought that he was very brave, one of the nurses could walk onto the ward at any time, and he would be caught, but he did not seem to care. I was so enthralled that I just continued to stare wide eyed at him and, I must admit, my mouth started to water. Then, suddenly, he looked over at me, and saw me staring. He pulled a grape from its stem and held it out to me.

"Here, would you like one?" he asked in a very hushed voice.

I shyly nodded.

"Yes please," I whispered, hoping and rather expecting him to come and bring the grape over to me.

But he didn't. Instead, he called over to me again.

"Quick, come and get it before someone comes back in," he whispered glancing around.

I looked up from the bunch of grapes to the boy, then across to the doors; from beyond I could hear the faint voices of the nurses and the muffled treads of footfalls echoing along the long corridors. I glanced back at the boy and shook my head.

The boy thought about it.

"Would you like me to throw it over for you?"

I nodded — yes.

He looked around him, making sure that the coast was clear, then crawled onto the top of the bed then he threw the grape towards me. Wide-eyed, I watched it sail through the air before landing right on the end of my bed.

Now my heart went in my mouth and as I stared at it lying there on my bed — I was horrified.

"Quick, get it!" he called over.

I looked at him rather despairingly, and he gestured with his hand towards the grape. I slowly, and rather reluctantly, pulled myself over the bed covers and reached out, but I couldn't reach the grape, it was too far away, so, I quickly positioned myself back into bed.

"Crawl onto the top of the bed," he called over to me in a very hushed voice. "You'll be able to get it then. It will be ok. If you are quick, they won't see you — quick hurry!"

Now I may have been young and, yes, I was rather shy, but I wasn't stupid. I knew that if I got caught on top of the bed trying to get a grape when I wasn't supposed to then I would be in a lot of trouble, and I certainly did not want that to happen! So, there was no way that I was going to crawl on top of the bed to get the grape. I looked over at him and shook my head.

The boy was, by now, getting quite desperate, knowing that if I did not pick up the grape and eat it, he would also be in trouble. He tried encouraging me. "Go on, it's ok. You can do it," he frantically called out to me.

But I completely froze, I could not do it. I looked at the grape then up at the boy, who must have seen the fear in my eyes.

He looked anxiously about, looking flustered. Then, he frantically jumped out of bed, his bare feet slapping the cold floor as he ran across over to my bed and quickly flicked the grape over to me, then he shot back into his own bed.

And me? Well, that grape had landed right onto my lap, and as I sat there beaming from ear to ear, I quickly picked it up and popped it right into my mouth. And my goodness! I did enjoy that rather tasty and juicy grape. I was so happy.

And the boy, he looked so relieved and rather flustered as he rested back upon his pillow. I was sure that he would not forget me in a hurry.

I have, throughout my life, often looked back upon that morning and it always brings a smile to my face. I have often wondered whatever became of him and if he remembers the little girl who had caused him so much stress that morning.

I know that I shall never forget, and will always remember him and that incident with fondness. And I certainly will never forget the day of my encounter with the boy with the grape.

CHAPTER ELEVEN
MY HOSPITAL ENCOUNTER

There are times when your mind will shut down and block out haunting memories from resurfacing, although a small fragment of what happened will linger, affecting you; growing up I had a fear of the dark, I had a fear of being alone.

This all stemmed from the time I spent at the hospital, and, although this all happened many, many years ago, I was always haunted by it, and always am.

I awake with a start.

Where am I?

I am in a strange place, and it is very dark and I am feeling disorientated, very confused and very frightened.

Something is happening to me, something which I do not understand, and I start whimpering; I try to move and lift my head up, but I can't — strong hands are roughly holding me down, making it extremely difficult for me to do so. My heart starts to hammer in my chest. Panic and fear built up and I start to cry out — I want my mum. But the person holding me down applies more pressure to stop me from squirming, and just holds me down even more firmly.

From somewhere above in the darkness a stern, cold voice tells me to keep still and to keep quiet, and to stop making such a fuss.

"It will all be over soon."

I am too young and afraid and I continue to squirm on the bed. I begin to feel immense pain and great discomfort as they begin their medical examination of me.

Or so I think.

Instead, I was being inappropriately touched.

My parents never got to find out about the abuse; I never told them, shutting it completely out of my mind. I cannot remember any other events that occurred thereafter in the hospital. I can only remember after that dreadful incident being at home and my mum putting some drops put into my eyes in the mornings. I have no recollections of what took place after that dreadful ordeal. I kept it hidden away, deep inside of me, just blank memories that I wanted forgotten.

The assault upon me that day went on to have a dramatic effect upon my life and even now, in my sixties, I am still afraid of the dark, and when I go to bed at night, I always have to have the curtains slightly open so that light comes into my room.

But I cannot change the past and what happened; life has to go on, I am so lucky I had wonderful parents, who cared and loved me, and who made me feel safe when I was at home with them. So yes, I count myself very lucky. You see, what I went through was nothing compared, to the dreadful, traumatic, cruel and unhappy childhood upbringing my mum had endured.

CHAPTER TWELVE
MUM

How lucky am I, having had the best Mum that anyone could ever wish for? She was generous, thoughtful and kind. She was also honest and very caring, and when she smiled all my troubles seem to suddenly just melt away. It was like the sun had come out, she looked absolutely radiant. She was truly the perfect Mum and she was the best.

Whenever I was unwell, upset, or hurt myself – falling over and scraping my knees – she was always there, lovingly tending to my injuries, giving me cuddles, and making me feel better. That was what Mum was like.

Mum liked to knit, and she often knitted clothes for my dolls and teddies during the evenings while watching the television, her long needles clicking away as she worked the coloured balls of wool

Every night she tucked me up in bed, making me feel secure and safe, always checking the dark corners of the bedroom to see that everything was ok before she left. And, in the mornings when I awoke and got out of bed and went downstairs, Mum would be there, making or preparing my breakfast, greeting me with a smile, a kiss and a hug while wishing me good morning. After breakfast, Mum would stand there and combe and plait my hair, before delicately tying the braids with pretty coloured ribbons.

Our family was expanding, but that did not mean our parents were too busy for us. Mum spent time with us; showed us love and affection, gave us attention. Often my sisters and I would sit gathered around our small black and white television set in our living room and watch the children's programmes that they had back in those days: *Watch With Mother*, *Andy Pandy, Blue Peter, The Sooty Show, The Wooden tops, Pinkie and Perky,* and *Flower Pot Men*.

Often Mum would watch with us, and I can remember one time when she sat down with us when *Blue Peter* was on. On the programme that day, one of the presenters, Valerie Singleton, was showing how you could make your very own merry-go-round using a cheese spread box. I watched fascinated and, after the programme had finished, I turned to Mum and told her that I thought it was really good what she had made; so, Mum replied that she would make one for me.

She took the last couple pieces of Dairy lea cheese out from the flat round box and proceeded to make a carousel out of bits and pieces that she had collected; Mum often kept aside small jam jars, cotton, rubbers, items which most people would have disregarded as rubbish, and she would find use for them, such as on that day. She worked hard and after she had finished, she came into the living room and showed my sisters and myself the end result. And I must confess, I was pretty amazed as it looked really good – brilliant in fact – and just like the one on *Blue Peter*.

I can't remember what the horses were made from, probably cardboard, but the carrousel looked lifelike, and you could even make it go around. Mum really did a good job on making that for me, and I can still picture that carousel, even now.

Although money was tight with all the mouths they had to feed, Mum always liked to make sure that we were smartly dressed, and that we wore clothes that were ideal for the summer and winter months. If we needed new clothes, such as dresses for the summer or cardigans for the winter, then they made sure they went ahead bought us new ones. I remember a time once when I was quite young when I had outgrown my winter coat. With the winter steadily approaching and a cold chill in the crisp morning air, Mum desperately needed to buy me a new coat, and I believe she ordered one for me at a local shop; most of which were independent back in those days, by paying in weekly or monthly instalments, as that was the only way she could afford it.

I can still see that moment when I received my new coat. It was very fluffy, a deep shade of red patterned with black markings. I really liked it and was absolutely thrilled that it had finely come, but when I put it on it was slightly too big and the sleeves hung over my hands. The coat was too long.

I remarked to Mum that it was too big, but she said that I would grow into it, and that at least my coat would last for a long while. I was rather happy in my new coat, and on the following Monday morning, feeling proud, I wore my oversized coat with pride as I made my way for school. Unfortunately, the other children were very unkind about my oversized coat, and I would be taunted rather badly over the following few months by those who found such amusement in teasing and mocked me daily in their spiteful glee at how ridiculous I looked. But although I dreaded their mocking's and teasing, I was grateful to Mum and Dad for spending their money on me so that I could keep warm, and I never told them of how much I was being picked on. And my coat would last me for the next few winters.

I can remember on another occasion Mum taking me down the road to buy me a new dress. Usually, outgrown clothing would be handed down to the younger siblings, but it was still necessary to go shopping on occasions. As money was tight, Mum never took us clothes shopping together, but would buy us what we needed individually. So, as I was now growing out of my other dresses, Mum had decided that it was time for me to have a new one. I can remember my excitement as I walked along beside Mum, holding her hand as we walked along the bustling high street; I do not know of which time of the year it was, or whether I wore a coat, but I believe the sun was shining, and I was extremely happy as I chatted away.

The shop seemed big to me, and as I gazed around at the dresses and clothes that were hanging from the rails, Mum spoke to the assistant, who went to the back of the shop to pick out some dresses for me to look at. She came back with two dresses which she held up for me to see; I stared at them both and then looked at Mum.

"Well Theresa, which one would you like? You can choose either one," Mum told me.

But the thing was, I liked them both and I couldn't decide which one to choose. I told Mum that I liked both and couldn't decide, and Mum explained that she could only afford to buy one dress, so I had to make my mind up. I must have stood there in that shop for absolutely ages, just looking at those two dresses, undecided and unable to pick out a dress.

By now both Mum and the shop assistant were getting tired of waiting for me to make up my mind and tried encouraging me, but to no avail. I suppose in some selfish way, I would have loved to have had both dresses, but that would not have been right, so in the end and much to the relieve of Mum and the rather bored looking shop assistant, I finally chose one which had a lovely silk ribbon tie belt. I can imagine that Mum must have been so relieved to have got out of that shop; and going home I remember of how pleased I was as I carried my new dress home.

*

Mum had her likes and dislikes; things which made her all the more unique to me. Her favourite colour was blue; she adored sweets like walnut whirls and sugared almonds, of which Dad, on the odd occasion, would buy her a bag.

She enjoyed baking, and we had cakes which us children would help to stir and prepare before being allowed to lick the leftovers from the spoon and bowl. She enjoyed listening to music and liked the then modern crooning by singers such as Frank Ifield and Roy Orbison. She liked to watch the London Palladium on our black and white television set every Sunday evening. She once told me how she would love to go and see the London Palladium show live on stage, but, sadly, she never did.

I can remember that, for years, she always applied Nivea cream to her face, a thing that she did daily, and throughout her life she always had a soft complexion. People often said that she always looked young for her age, and that is something that I certainly agree with.

Sometimes, on rare occasions, Mum would wear lipstick; usually whenever she had the chance to go out, and sometimes at home, just because she felt like it. And I remember once, when I was young and inquisitive, sitting in her bedroom watching her intently as she first powdered her face and then started to apply her lipstick, asking her why she was doing it. She replied that it made her feel good, but she didn't do it often because Dad didn't like her wearing makeup.

"Why?" I asked, my legs swinging from the end of her bed. She told me that Dad had told her that she didn't need to cover her face in make-up, that she looked alright as she was. And as I continued watching her doing her face, I told her that I thought she looked very nice, whether she was wearing makeup or not, and she turned away from the mirror, and gave me an affectionate hug.

There was the one thing which Mum disliked more than anything and that was thunderstorms. In fact, her dislike for them was so bad that she lived in total fear of them.

She absolutely hated the storms, and this fear soon grew in me and my siblings too. I can remember many times during the nights when lightning crackled across the dark sky and thunder growled so loudly that our house seemed to shake. My sisters and I would all jump out of our beds in fright and run into Mum and Dad's bedroom and to the safety under their warm bedcovers. Dad would get out of bed and leave the bedroom and wait until the storm had passed, then, when we had all rather reluctantly gone back to our own beds, he would then go back to bed himself.

But there was truly a very bad incident that I will never, ever forget. It happened one Sunday morning when Dad had gone down to his local, and Mum had been cooking the roast dinner and looking after us all as we played happily in the living room.

The weather suddenly turned rather bad. Clouds, heavy and dark, rolled over the sky and specks of lightning ignited the sky; swirls of rain, which started to fall in large, heavy drops, pattered against the windowpanes. Despite her fear, Mum usually coped well, especially as we were in the safety of our home, but this storm developed into what they called a valley storm, a storm which is harsh and usually quite long lasting.

And soon, as the rain lashed against the windows and rapped against the door, and the lightning tore up the sky, igniting the rooms in our house in flames of blue. We began to scream our heads off; we were all petrified, and we all frantically huddled around Mum, who was just as scared as we all were. Thunderbolts roared overhead so loudly that our house seemed to shake, and our petrified screams were soon to be drowned out.

We were so distressed that I can remember of someone in the family literally banging on the wall out of pure fear. Mum was desperately hoping and praying that Dad would come home, but he didn't return until after closing time.

I cannot remember of how long the storm lasted, I only know that it seemed to go on forever, before it suddenly eased off, when poor Mum, who was feeling frightened and nervous herself, was able to calm all of us terrified children down. I do remember that when Dad did eventually come home, he was surprised to find us all nervous and huddled up with Mum.

Mum was really so upset with him. And what made it so much worse was when she asked him why he hadn't bothered to come home, knowing full well of how afraid we all were of storms, and this one being such a particularly bad one.

To her utter dismay Dad just looked calmly at her and casually remarked, "Oh, I thought you were all alright."

*

One of Mum's favourite pastimes was baking. I can remember times when I wasn't playing with my sisters, when I would sit and watch as she prepared and cooked dinners or lunches, and we would talk and chat to each other as she did so.

Mum loved to make cakes whenever she got the time, and I can remember on one occasion she made a really scrumptious chocolate cake; she sandwiched the two sponges together with a thick layer of chocolate cream between, then spread it thickly with chocolate icing. It looked great!

We would all sit around the table having had our tea, and eagerly wait for Mum to cut us all a slice of her rather mouth-watering cake, watching her intently as she did so. And when I was finally handed my plate with that chocolate cake on it, I eagerly picked it up and took my first bite; it tasted really good, and I just couldn't stop telling Mum of how delicious it was. As there was so many of us in the family, a cake didn't go far, so there was only one slice for each of us, but it was the best cake that I had ever tasted in my life.

Mum was never one for getting into fights or arguments. She was always a very quiet and placid person who always got on with everybody and, like Dad, was very well liked and respected by our neighbours and community. She had a sweet and pleasant nature, and basically got on with everybody and would always try to avoid any confrontation. But my mum could retaliate, if anyone was to really upset her, or run her or her children down; then that was when Mum would have words with them.

She was always so protective of us, and she would never lose her temper, but she was never afraid of confronting anyone no matter who or how big they were, whether they be a man or a woman.

I can remember one such occasion when I was walking home from school. As I started walking down our road, I could hear a lot of commotion. Eager to find out what was going on, I started to hurry towards home as fast as I could. And it was as I neared home that it dawned on me that one of the angry, arguing voices was that of my mum.

With horror I hurried homewards, to find Mum and our next-door neighbour having a very heated argument. I do not know what had actually happened or what had been said that had obviously upset Mum so much, but I do know that it was something to do with me and my siblings, for Mum was defending us from the wrongdoings our neighbour was accusing us of. As I have mentioned, Mum was very protective of her children and she did not tolerate anyone saying anything unkind or bad about us. So, whatever our neighbour had said really made Mum very upset

I can remember the neighbour hadn't liked Mum answering her back, telling Mum that she would call the police, and Mum telling her to go ahead then, and call the police she didn't care! This caused our neighbour to become even more enraged, and I was sure that they were going to start an actual fight over the fence.

I stood there listening to the two of them arguing with each other, growing more fearful with each and every insult and accusation and poke of the finger. I tried to get Mum away, pulling on her dress, but she was not budging and stood her ground. Instead she gently shoved me out of the way and ordered me indoors, and I rather reluctantly moved away from them as she continued to stick up for herself. I was so relieved when Mum, after having the last word, finally moved away from the fence, and came inside the house.

I have never forgotten about that incident, I believe because Mum had stuck up for the family, defending herself and her children. For years after that dreadful incident my mum and our neighbour got on very well with each other, and our neighbour once even gave me and my siblings a box full of 78rpm records so that when we were outside in our back garden, we could play them on our wind-up gramophone.

I very much admired my mum; she always fought her own battles and never got my dad involved. She always stood her ground and defended her family, and I am proud of her for this, and I grew up having had a lot of respect for her. What I also admired about her was that she was never afraid to stick up for herself or for what was right, and she never backed down.

My sisters and I often reminisce about our childhood and the gifts of memories we share of growing up in our house on Spreighton Road. We often recall those times we shared – celebrations, family gatherings and other antics – with both amusement and laughter. And also, with gratitude that we were part of those times; that we lived, saw and shared those treasured memories from those times long ago when our family were still young and before it grew so big. Memories we treasured with warmth and a deep sadness as the years had rolled by, distancing us with each passing season from those times.

And it was on one of these occasions that my sister told me about the time that Mum had stood up to one of Dad's friends who he bought back from the pub one Sunday. This chap had wanted to meet Mum, but unfortunately the visit was very short. As both Dad and his friend had rather had one too many to drink, they were in a rather giggly mood and, for a laugh, this friend went and sat on Jenny's stool. Mum and Dad had brought Jenny a desk and chair for the Christmas just gone, and it had not been all that long ago, so the desk and chair was still quite new. However, the chair was only a child's size and was not sturdy enough to hold an adult's weight. So, this chap sat himself down on Jenny's chair for a giggle and completely smashed it. Although I was much too young to have remembered this, going by what my sister said, Mum flew at him and chased him right out of the house. This chap later told my dad that he would never again set foot inside our house again, as Mum had terrified him. But that was Mum, and who could blame her for being so cross?

I can remember many years' later Mum standing up and defending herself against a young lad who was threatening her with a knife. She just calmly stood her ground, casually picked up an empty milk bottle, smashed it against a brick wall and held it up in front of her — daring him to even try. Needless to say, he soon realized that he was picking on the wrong person and he very quickly turned and ran off.

Mum was so well-liked and kind, but one thing she never talked much about was of her childhood. She told us stories about herself as a teenager working in an office, and of her time in WAAF during WWII, including amusing stories of how they were based on a haunted airfield. But she never spoke much about her childhood, and I would soon learn why.

CHAPTER THIRTEEN
MUM'S LOST CHILDHOOD

I can remember that day so very well. It was one gloriously hot day and the sun was shining brightly, lighting up our kitchen with its glare. I was sitting at the table watching as Mum prepared the dinner.

We were talking, as we often did about various things, Mum answering and feeding my knowledge as she worked while I sat there, and it suddenly occurred to me that I had never seen or knew anything of my Nan and granddad from her side of the family.

"Mum, why have I never seen your Mum and Dad," I asked curiously. "Why don't they come round to see us?"

Mum stopped what she was doing and turned to me.

"Because they are not around anymore," she told me quietly, and being so young and innocent to the world around me, I asked where they were. Mum replied that they had died a long time ago.

I felt very saddened to learn that, for I could not imagine losing my mum at such a young age; but I was also inquisitive to find out about my mum's hidden side of the family. I asked if she missed them very much, and Mum replied that she had never known them. She came over and sat across from me and explained to me as softly as she could that she had been told that her Mum had died very shortly after she was born, and that her Dad had died just a few years later. As she had been so young at the time, she harboured no memories of her parents — she never knew them or even what they had looked like.

"Who looked after you then?" I asked. "While you were growing up whom did you live with? An aunt then?"

"No, I didn't have any family who could look after me."

"So, you were left all on your own then?" I asked her in disbelief.

"I had a brother, Thomas. He was a year older than me, and all we had was each other." Mum talked a little about her brother and how there just wasn't any relatives that were able to take them in. It was very upsetting hearing about this, how my mum had no parents that loved and cared for her, not at all like how she was always there for me, and how lonely she must have been. I asked what happed then, if she had no aunts or uncles that were alive who could have taken them in.

"We were put into foster care," Mum replied, explaining that since she and Thomas were both orphans their care was placed with the local council who, in turn, sent them to live with a foster family.

I was delighted about this and told her so, but then Mum told me something that I found quite shocking and disturbing.

"Oh no, Theresa," she replied rather bitterly. "They didn't take me in out of love or kindness, or because they cared; they only fostered because they got paid for taking children in."

Mum went on to explain the harsh upbringing she had endured while going from one foster home to another. No matter what home she and her brother found themselves placed in, their foster parents were always rather uncaring, unloving and sometimes rather dreadful. Beatings were quite common, even for the smallest of things.

Mum explained about a time when a plate of cakes had been left in her reach. She had been told not to take any of them, but had been left unattended for a long while and the temptation had been too much for her, and she had taken a cake. Unfortunately, she had been caught eating it by her foster mother, who had been very livid. Mum had been severely punished; she was smacked then dragged to a cupboard, where she was forcefully pushed in, and then the door was slammed closed and locked. Mum was left in the dark for quite some period of time before she was eventually allowed out.

Mums only possession, apart from her clothing, was a doll which she absolutely treasured. Every foster child had their own clothing and personal items, such as her doll, and Mum kept it with her as often as she could. Sometimes, she was forbidden to play with her doll, so it was mostly kept in her bedroom at the bottom of her bed.

I am now unsure which foster carers Mum was with at the time, or of her age, as she never said, but as she was leaving with her bag of belongings and with her doll held firmly in her arms to transfer to another foster carer suddenly her doll was snatched from her arms by her former foster parent, who unkindly told her that she was not allowed to take her doll with her.

Needless to say, Mum was very, very upset, but had no choice but to leave her precious doll behind.

Despite my young age, I could understand why Mum never spoke much about her past, for I could see that she never grew up experiencing the joys of a mother's love, something I was so grateful to experience myself. But, looking back at that time, I knew that Mum's ruined, loveless childhood had made her a much stronger and a much better person. On another occasion when her past was bought up again, she told me that she once vowed that if she ever got married, and had children of her own, she would never ever treat them in the way that she had been treated herself. And she didn't.

She kept her word and we were bought up in a loving, warm and welcome home that was filled with security; a home that was full of love. Throughout my life she gave me so much encouragement and knowledge and taught me that I could go on and achieve or be anything that I wanted to be, and most of all she taught me to always believe in myself.

Mum had always brought such warmth into my life, and she enriched the lives of my brothers and sisters with heaps of love, so learning of her traumas, of her growing up in care shocked us all. She had given us all such a warm and stable home life — something she had never had. To us, we were her world and Mum worked tirelessly to give us a good childhood, something which she herself had been denied.

The sad thing is that, much later – just before she died – Mum found out that she had an aunt who was still alive, and it was Mum's wish to try and trace her. I think Mum would have liked to have known about her parents, about who they were, what they had looked like, and why the aunt herself had distanced herself from them. She had many questions which desperately needed answering but, sadly, for Mum it was too late for her to find the answers.

*

Violet Rosina Wheatley came into the world on a bitterly cold, frosty day in 1925, on Wednesday 25th November just as the sounds of the bow bells could be heard ringing. She was born at her family home at number 7 Donald Street, a line of working-class houses that outlined the slums of Bow & Bromley in the London district of Poplar, where the air hung thick with the smoke which curled from the chimneys and rang to the sounds of ships coming into dock.

Her mother was Florence Eliza Crookes, a widower when both Mum and Thomas were born, and who already had two older children – Arthur and Florence – from her previous marriage to her late husband, Arthur Wheatley Senior.

Mum and Thomas, lived with their mother and older siblings in that house. It is not known if there was anyone else living there. Her mother, who had been very ill, suddenly died on the 21st December 1930. Mum and her brother were then registered as orphans.

It is unclear why Mum's older siblings never took her and her brother on permanently. But Mum and Thomas were kept in their sister's care until they were transferred to the local authority, from where, in accordance with the Poor Law Act of 1930, they would be placed into children's homes and foster care until the age of eighteen.

My mum and Thomas were placed into the care of the council on the 24th February 1931 and were then moved into Langley House, which was a receiving home, orphanage and workhouse. Mum, at the time of her mother's death, had been attending the Marnet Street LCC infant school, but upon being taken into the care of the council, it was then requested that she should be transferred from her school and be placed at Hutton Residential School in Essex. Hutton Residential School was known to house many orphaned children from the overcrowded London orphanage, and while their Mum had to spend a considerable time at the Eastern Hospital after she contracted measles.

After Mum was discharged from hospital on the 23rd August 1932, she and her brother were declared fit by the authorities and they were then placed into their first foster home, which was located in Ditching, Sussex, where they were under the care of a Mr and Mrs Rowland. From here on Mum's childhood became very strict, harsh and more traumatic. Both she and Thomas were often punished, even for the minor offensives, and they grew up never having been shown any affection.

Time living with the Rowland family was short and, on 19th October 1933, Mum once again packed up whatever few clothes that she had, along with her favourite doll, and moved into a second foster home, located seven miles away in Hassocks. This time their foster carer was a Mrs Collins.

Mum's stays in foster care were often short, as if to make her and her brother feel unwelcome. Often travelling by train, Mum and her brother would be burdened with their small sack of belongings and paperwork, including a list of clothing, which would be handed to the new carer. It was customary for all fostered children to have their clothing listed, as the council paid extra money towards any clothing a child needed. Mum and her brother remained in care together until Thomas came of age.

They continued living in Hassocks for the next couple of years, until, at the age of ten they found themselves suddenly being transferred out of Sussex and relocating to Epsom, Surrey to live under the care of their third foster carer, a Mrs Eliza Marks and her husband, Billy, who was a retired gardener. They were both in their sixties when they fostered Mum and her brother, who remained under the roof of the Marks household on Lower Court Road from 12th December 1935 until just over a year later. Then once again London County Council transferred both children back to London where, on 1st January 1937, they were placed with a Mrs Robson. By now Mum was eleven years old and she remained in the care of the Robson family until 5th February 1942.

Despite the frequent moving around and living in care, Mum still had to have an education and attend school. Mum was a good writer and excellent at spelling and the one thing she really loved doing whilst in care was playing netball at school — she once told me that it was something that she had really loved participating in.

With her brother Thomas now out working, Mum attended school while living under Mrs Robson's care, and although still in care she moved into the Salvation Army hostel in Clapham in May 1942.

But Mum struggled to fit in at the hostel, as she felt it was rather restrictive. So she found a job working in the office of Gloy Adhesives – a job which she was reportedly happy with – in a small estate in Devonshire Square, a fair distance from the hostel. In October that year she made the move out of the hostel, encouraged by her support worker and after a friend had recommended her, moved in with a Mrs Andrews in Tottenham. But unfortunately Mum did not have a good time there and was not happy, and it was reported on record that she wished that she could move out.

Finally, on her eighteenth birthday, in 1943, Mum was discharged from care. She was now a free young woman.

Mum then went and joined the Women's Auxiliary Air Force, better known as Women's Royal Air Force, where she remained for the duration of the war. Mum once told my sisters and I that it was the best time of her life, and she had many stories that she shared with me.

After the war, Mum found herself settled in Weymouth, Dorset, and became employed as a domestic servant in Wesley Street, with a family called Dobbs. She remained there until 1947, when she moved away and settled down in Molesey to live with her brother Thomas and his wife. That was where a new life would begin for Violet.

In late 1941 an aunt, who was the sister of her late mother, had written to the council enquiring as to the health and wellbeing of my mum and her brother. I find it incredibly sad that my mum never knew about this aunt until shortly before she died. And I find it heartbreaking to think that, for reasons unbeknown to us, she was abandoned by her family, a family that she never knew she had.

CHAPTER FOURTEEN
A TRADITIONAL ROMANY DISH

As my parents had a lot of mouths to feed, and money was tight, Mum would often provide us with cooked meals that would go around for everyone. Once a week (I believe on a Monday) she would cook a stew for our dinner. She would always go down to the butcher that very day and buy some neck of mutton, as it was cheap and economical. Back in those days a lamb or a beef joint was inexpensive to buy.

I remember often watching Mum as she cooked and prepared the stew, savouring the delightful smell of the meat simmering in the saucepan along, with the vegetables, the onions and carrots, and then the dumplings and gravy. It always tasted delicious and was extremely filling. And best of all it went around and fed a large family.

Another meal that I loved and was also economical was Mum's homemade spam fritters, which was made up using slices of round luncheon meat. Mum would mix some batter in a bowl then dip the meat in one at a time to coat it thickly with batter before transferring it into a hot frying pan. Mum would then fry each one, turning them over so both sides cooked and were golden. When they were done, she would serve them with mashed or boiled potatoes and some veg, along with deliciously hot gravy. It was a meal that I really liked and it was a cheap and simple dinner for Mum to make.

There were so many meals that Mum cooked for us, such as a toad in the hole or sausage and mash; all filling meals that went around to feed a large and hungry family. Mum also made her own made steak and kidney puddings which she used to steam in large pots on the stove, and she made fantastic rice puddings, which had crispy brown skin on the top. After she served us each a spoon of pudding into our dish, we would pour some carnation milk onto the top. It was lovely.

Mum worked hard in the kitchen to feed her family, and I remember the sweet treats she used to bake for us such as her cakes and shortbreads; and I remember nibbling her homemade coconut ice, the sweet texture of it is mouth-watering even now. Once she undertook the almighty task of making some homemade jam using real strawberries, and she would make sugared dumplings for our tea, serving these on a plate with strawberry jam. Sometimes she would also make her own apple and blackberry pies, which were very tasty and delicious.

Mum had so many mouths to feed and was always very busy, but she always made sure that we had plenty to eat, and no matter how tired she felt she would be standing in front of the stove cooking for me and the rest of the family. So, one day, I was rather surprised when my dad suddenly announced that he would be cooking us all a dinner.

I don't remember why my dad was cooking a meal that day. But I remember that I had ventured into the kitchen and was rather astonished to see him getting the frying pan out from the cupboard and placing it on the stove. Dad must have seen the surprise look upon my face, because he went on to explain to me that he was going to cook something special for us all. He went on to tell me that it was a special dish that his Mum used to cook for him and his family.

I asked him what it was and he explained that it was a traditional Romany dish. Dad often told us about his Romany roots; of living in horse-drawn wagons and by what the land provided; stories we had disbelieved when we were so young. It was only later I learned that what Dad cooked for us that day was called a Joey Grey. This was a common meal for travelling families, offering nourishment and warmth all at a low cost. It is said that the meal came about after a starving traveller who had hit on bad times and was in desperate need of food went and collected all the little vegetables that he could find and placed them into a pan which he boiled up over a fire. This dish would go on to serve the Romany community well and was rightly named after Joey Grey.

And, that day I watched intently as Dad got to work. He got a few potatoes which he peeled and sliced before placing them in the pan. He got a couple of onions and proceeded to do the same as he did with the potatoes, and then put in tomatoes. Dad poured water into the pan, just enough to cover all the ingredients, and then he allowed it to slowly simmer until it was nice and tender. You can add bacon or sausages and gravy into the pan as well, and a Joey Grey can be served with bread and butter.

There was enough to go around for everyone and Dad served up the food and placed the plates before us as we sat around the kitchen table. I must confess that what Dad cooked that day smelt and tasted so good, and it is something that I always remember. I certainly will never forget the day that my dad cooked us a true traditional Romany dish.

CHAPTER FIFTEEN
MY ROMANY GRANDPARENTS

I treasured the time I got to spend with my granddad; the family gatherings at his house and at Christmas were always a magical time for me and the memories I have of such times will last me forever.

My grandad, Joseph Ayres, met and married my Nan, Dorothy Howard, on 12th June 1920 at the parish church in Walton-on-Thames, Surrey, where they spoke their vows and left their mark on the registry. At the time both families had been encamped close by at Broadlane Farm, which must have been a popular place for Romany travellers to stop at and to find work.

Granddad worked for a while as a farm labourer, a job he had experience in due to working on farms during his youth. I have no idea of how long they stayed at the farm, or where they went when they did eventually leave, but I believe that my grandparents often returned to Broadlane Farm, as, five years later, my dad was born there. Albert was their third child, and like his siblings before him, he was born in the horse drawn wagon, or vardo (as is the proper name for a Romany wagon), which they called home.

When it was time to eventually move on, my grandparents, along with my dad and their other children, left the farm, and continued to make their way in the direction of Molesey. It was around 1927 that the local council were building houses in Spreighton Road.

In the 1920s the country was still recovering from the aftermath of the First World War, as well as from the effects of the Spanish flu, and there were many ex-service men who had been injured during the conflict and had nowhere to call home. The government had pledged to build houses, which councils would own, and which originally were known 'Homes for Heroes', or simply council houses. During this time there were a lot of Romany travellers in the southeast, working the farms and lands which had been left unattended due to the number of working men lost due to the war and then the pandemic.

Council officials visited members of the Romany community to offer homes, and my grandparents were offered one of the houses on Spreighton Road, giving them a chance of settling down. Or they could move on their way. My grandparents decided that it would be better for them and their children to settle down to a new way of life. So, they took up the offer of one of the houses and moved into their new home and to a new way of life for the remainder of their lives.

They were the first Romany family to have been offered a council house.

Although my grandparents settled down, it was not at all easy at first, especially for my Nan, who found it hard to adapt and missed the Romany way of life. She continued with the traditions that she was accustomed too, and I often heard stories of her causing quite a stir.

Following the birth of my dad, another five children would be born to my grandparents. And whenever my Nan had a new baby, she would think nothing of sitting on the front doorstep breastfeeding in full view of all her neighbours. She simply did not have a care in the world.

Nan would also busy herself by making pegs and then going around the houses selling them. She also sold small sprigs of heather that she had tied into little bunches, earning herself a bit of money. I think she used to try to keep, not forget, her Romany ways.

Unfortunately I never knew my grandmother as she died when I was only about two years old, but I can remember my grandfather very well. He was quite the family man, who was always smartly dressed, always wearing a waistcoat.

He had an accordion and would, on certain occasions when we would all go around to my grandparents' house; play so that he could entertain us all. He liked all the family to get together that was the type of man he was. I have many happy memories of sitting there watching and listening to him play. He would stand there in the middle of the room, with his family all around him. I was absolutely mesmerised, listening to the different kinds of music that he played. I simply loved those special moments. This is something that I will never forget, visions that I still have of my granddad standing there tall and proud, playing on his accordion.

As we lived so near to my grandparents, my parents would take me and my siblings over to visit them often. And I can remember on one such occasion, when we had gone around, of me venturing out into their back garden.

It was a lovingly kept garden, with a wonderful array of flowers. As you wandered up the garden path, halfway along, before you reached the top of the garden, stood a trellis or wooden archway which was adorned by roses. They grew up the sides and over the top of this archway, and it was absolutely beautiful.

Being so young, I remember walking through it, thinking as I did so, of how delightful it looked, and how the fragrant smell of the roses was delightful. It was a wondrous feature to their garden, and to me truly magical. My grandparents took such pride of their house, home and garden.

After my grandparents had settled into their new way of life, my grandfather found work and provided for his steadily growing family. He had three sons. The youngest was Henry who sadly passed away at the tender age of two, dying in his father's arms. It was said that in his grief my granddad said that his son was, "Far too good for this life."

My Nan continued having children late in life, and the last Ayres child to be born to my grandparents was in 1939 when my Nan gave birth to a daughter called Junie. My mother once told me that when Junie was born, they found out from the doctor that she had Down syndrome. In those days such children were referred to as Mongols and their life expectancy was unnaturally short — the doctor said that Junie would not live past the age of twenty. Then he told my grandparents that it was best if she be taken away from them and placed in an institution.

My grandparents, I was told, were aghast at the doctor's suggestion, and were quite angry with him. Mum told me that my grandfather told him straight that she was their daughter, and there was no way that they were going to give her up. She was staying with them. There was definitely no way that she was to be placed in a home.

That was their Romany way, families stayed together, and they would bring her up just like the rest of their children. And they did.

My grandparents treated Junie just like their other children, and when Nan passed away it was left to Granddad to look after her, and a strong bond was formed between father and daughter. Sadly, Granddad died in 1966, and then Junie was then cared for by my aunt and uncle, who lived nearby.

My older sister Jennifer had developed quite a bond with Junie. And whenever she had one of her tantrums – you could hear her screaming and shouting and slamming doors, from their house to ours – she seemed to be the only one to be able to communicate with her and calm her down. And before long, as was expected, my uncle would come around to ask Mum and Dad if Jenny could go around; and as soon as she got there and spoke to Junie, she would stop, happy that my sister was with her. This happened on many an occasion, and every time it was only my sister Jenny that could calm Junie down.

Jenny thought so much of Junie that, many years later when my sister was getting married, she was the only one to have ever invited Junie to her wedding reception. I can remember that day very well, and of how emotional my sister was of having her there, and of the big cuddles and hugs that Junie kept giving her.

Unfortunately, years later it became hard caring for Junie, as my aunt and uncle had their own children to look after, and as her temperament was very fragile, it was decided Junie should be placed in a home, something my grandfather had been so against. But thankfully, homes had steadily improved, and Junie ended up being cared for with respect and she lived a much longer life then the twenty years the doctors had said.

No doubt, Granddad's passing had left a hole in our lives, but the stories and memories he left behind were truly grand, though sometimes sad.

During WWI, Granddad volunteered to fight for his country, but he was taken prisoner and treated rather badly, which affected him throughout his life. He suffered terrible nightmares because of his time as a POW, and he would often end up shouting in his sleep.

During WW2, I heard that he would – whenever the sirens went off or even as the bombs were being dropped – stand by the doorway of the air raid shelters that were located on the green across Walton Road from Spreighton Road. He would always make sure that every man, woman and child got into the safety of the shelter before he himself went in, and as the bombs blasted the ground, my grandfather kept spirits high.

He was a truly remarkable man, and a true gentleman. To me he was quite the hero.

CHAPTER SIXTEEN
THOSE DREADED SCHOOL DAYS

If there was one thing that I dreaded more than anything in the world; it was school. I absolutely hated it! And even now, just thinking about the unpleasant experiences I endured fills me with dread. It brings back nothing but very bad memories which continue to have a damaging impact upon my life. There was one particular incident, which now seems such a very long time ago, which left me absolutely afraid to interact with or socialize with my peers, or to even stick up for myself. And throughout the rest of my school years, I became painfully shy and timid, which made me an easy target for bullies to poke fun at, and to humiliate. And there was absolutely nothing that I could do to prevent any of this from happening, which left me feeling vulnerable and threatened.

I suppose I felt exactly the same every day that I went to school, that feeling of complete loneliness and intense isolation.

I cannot remember exactly what my first day at school was like, as my memory is now very vague about it, and there are only certain things that occurred during my schooling that are still quite vivid in my mind.

The first school that I attended, when I was about five years old, was the Sunnymead Infant School in Molesey.

Every morning Mum would walk me to school and stand by my side in the playground waiting for the bell to ring. She would give me a quick hug and a kiss, and tell me that she would see me later, and then she would wait as I made my way in through the school door. I would always glance back timidly and we would wave to each other. And then how I would hate it, when I saw Mum walking away to go home. I so longed to go home with her, but I could not do so.

I can remember as I walked through the school corridors, which to me seemed terribly long and very frightening, being shuffled and shoved from all sides by the hordes of children rushing around, all eager to not be late into class, all of us heading in the same direction towards the cloakroom. The sounds of chattering and laughing – and even crying – seemed to echo around the narrow school corridor. I can remember lingering awhile until the groups of children had subsided before entering the cloakroom. Each child had been assigned a peg in which to hang their coat on.

I can still remember some of our lessons. When we did our sums, we were given coloured wooden blocks of different lengths and sizes. I used to love putting them together and learning my numbers, I think that it really helped me with my sums. We also used to be given reading cards that had a picture at the top, and then had the few lines to read about Dick and Dora — a sample of a story written on them to help encourage you to read. We used to have to go up to the teacher's desk one at a time and read the words out to her. If you read well, you got praised, if you didn't you were given the card back and told to go back to your desk and to practice some more.

School back then in the Sixties was so different than today; it was a different regime then. Teachers were very strict and harsh, and you were confined to your desk, only getting up from your seat if you were asked to do so. The only time that you spoke to a teacher was to answer a question or if they spoke to you. The teachers wouldn't think twice about giving you a slap on the leg if they felt that you deserved it, even for the smallest of reasons.

Remembering this brings to mind an experience I had coming back to school after having been ill. I can remember that day so well. I had returned back to school and was feeling quite happy and well and we were all seated at our desks and I was listening to our teacher discussing about some work that had been done. Our teacher – a tall rather large woman who was very strict - picked up some school exercise book from a pile that she had on her desk and started to call out the pupil's names. And the first book on the pile just so happened to be mine.

"Theresa Ayres," she loudly called out my name, and I nervously got up from my seat and made my way over to her, watched in complete silence by the others in my class. As I had not been at school for a few days, I thought there couldn't be anything for me to worry about. But as I reached her desk, she rather suddenly pulled me to her side and, without any warning, lifted my skirt up slightly and gave me a very hard slap several times on the back of my leg.

It took me completely by surprise because I had never been hit at school before and it took all the strength that I could muster to not break down and cry. It really hurt and as I stood there before her, I could feel my leg burning and stinging. I was totally shocked by the punishment and I could feel my face going red and tears springing to my eyes; how I stopped myself from actually breaking down crying, I shall never know.

I could see the shocked and startled looks on the faces of the other children in the classroom as I was given a forceful telling off by the teacher before she ordered me to return to my desk. Shocked, dumbfounded and struggling to withhold my emotions, I rather shakily hurried back to my desk, feeling all the other children's eyes watching me as I did so. Meanwhile our teacher called up the next child by name. I kept wondering during the rest of the day what on earth I had done to have warranted such physical punishment.

And I decided that from now on I was going to be very wary indeed, if my name was to ever be called out again; by any one of my teachers. But if I thought that incident was the worst I would ever experience, then I was wrong — there was one particular teacher who was so cold and heartless towards me that she left me terrified and in absolute fear of her.

CHAPTER SEVENTEEN
THE TEACHER FROM HELL

Before our morning break, we would all sit crossed-legged on the floor while our teacher read a story to us. Now I liked trying to read from my books, but I never really listened to what the teacher was reading, so I used to sit there quite bored, just wanting the time to go so that I could have my bottle of milk and go out to play.

I would so often go off in a daydream, or just fidget; it was like that most times until the teacher finished the story that she had been reading. Then she would then put down her book and stare across at us all, ready to select one of us for an important job.

"Now, who shall I pick today to hand the straws around?" and everyone's hand in the classroom would automatically go up, including mine, each child eager and desperately wanting and hoping for the teacher to choose them. Throughout my years at infant school, I would always put up my hand, desperately making eye contact with the teacher, practically begging for her just for once to pick me. But no — sadly, I never did get chosen. The teacher always ignored me; I guess I just wasn't good enough in her eyes, not even to be able to hand around a box of drinking straws to the other children in her class.

This teacher's dislike towards me was so very obvious; of all the children in her class I was the only one never to have been selected. And unfortunately, looking back now, I feel that I must have been victimised because of an incident that had occurred when I had first started school.

The school used to supply the children with biscuits which were given to you when you had your milk; but they weren't free. You would have to give the teacher some money when the milk was handed out in exchange for your biscuits. I cannot remember if we had many choices to select from, but sometimes they had chocolate fingers. Nor can I remember if we had biscuits every day, or just once a week. But I remember Mum giving me money for my biscuits and I remember that I used to eat one with my milk and the other I used to always save to take home for my two-year-old sister. It was something I always looked forward to — before that incident.

As I have already mentioned, the teachers back in those days were very firm and strict. And it was the same with this teacher, whose name I shall not print. I can recall that she was very strict, and she hardly ever smiled and was always very distant towards me. For reasons I can only guess, she seemed to take a dislike to me, and I suppose – looking back now – that was because of my quiet nature. But during her care (and all through my schooling) I always behaved myself, as I was taught to by my parents. I never spoke during lessons unless I was spoken too, and I always made sure that I was always polite when answering the teacher's questions. Now at first, I coped rather well with being at school, even though I found it rather daunting being away from home. Until that day which was to change me, giving me an intense fear of her throughout my childhood.

The day in question started off as normal. After Mum had finished brushing my hair and getting me ready for school, she handed me a thruppenny bit so that I could buy some biscuits to have with my milk. I remember that I wore a light blue coloured jacket and, as Mum walked me to school, she told me to not lose my money, but to keep hold of it. So, after Mum had dropped me off, I remembered what she had told me, and I carefully put my money into one of my pockets to keep it safe.

Now in our classroom we had a type of cabinet that had small square partitions. Each child was allocated a square box to store our possessions in, such as our reading cards or our biscuit money. But that day I had decided it would be best to keep my money safe in my pocket.

When the teacher had finally finished reading her story, and had selected one child from the mass of waving arms for the important straw duty, she told us all to clear away our stuff to prepare to have our milk and biscuits, while she pulled out a packet of biscuits ready for the children who had bought money in.

I took out my money from my pocket, and holding it firmly in my hand, I went to join the queue. There was a girl in my class named Lizzie Dawson who was always very bossy towards me and the other children in the class. So I often tried to avoid her as best as I could. But that morning Lizzie had seen me taking my money out from my pocket, and as I made my way towards the milk crate to join the end of the queue, she stepped in front of me and barred my way. I could see by the look in her face that there was going to be trouble.

"Give me your money," she demanded, and held out her hand, waiting for me to give her my money.

But I refused, shaking my head. I may have been shy, but I certainly was not going to give that girl my money. Besides, she had her own money; I had seen her put it in her box earlier that morning.

"Give it to me!" she insisted again, this time trying to snatch the money from my hand.

"No," I said, and gently pushed her away. Now there was absolutely no way that I was going to give in to her threats and demands.

Lizzie was not at all happy and became very angry "You won't get away with this," she fumed as she walked away.

I watched her as she walked towards her box to get her money out. Sighing with relief, I joined the end of the queue, feeling rather pleased with myself for having actually stood up to Lizzie.

But my joy was short lived.

I noticed that Lizzie had made her way over to the teacher's desk at the front and was talking to her. Suddenly the teacher got up rather abruptly from her desk with a look of fury on her face.

"Theresa Ayres, what's this I hear about you stealing money?"

The class went silent. Everyone froze, all eyes watching.

I couldn't move, I stood there completely terrified, watching as she strolled over to where I stood, her eyes blazing. She leaned over me and I felt absolutely petrified.

Lizzie stood beside her with a smug expression on her face.

"Lizzie here says that you have taken her money from her box. Is that true? Answer me!"

"No," I whispered.

By now all the other children had gathered around the teacher, all quietly watching and wanting to know what was going on.

"Yes, she did! I saw her doing it. Look! She has it on her," Lizzie spoke up rather convincingly. I shook my head no, to terrified to even speak out against this wicked accusation.

"Show me your hand, now!" She grabbed my arm roughly and I had no choice but to open my hand and to reveal my money laying there in my palm.

"It's mine!" I tried protesting, but the teacher was livid and beyond reasoning; before her was a victim on whom she could unleash her rage.

"You wicked girl!" she shouted. "Stealing from another child."

"But this is my money," I said, starting to feel terribly upset at this dreadful ordeal that I was going through. "My mum gave it to me."

I tried to explain to her what had happened but it was no use. I was too shy and absolutely petrified of trying to defend myself. And, as usual, the teacher was not at all interested in listening to me or takes any notice of me defending myself or of my innocence.

And, to make things much worse and harder for me, Lizzie was far from finished either.

"Look, Miss," Lizzie took the teacher over to my box, with everyone following in a swarm.

"Look, Miss! There is Theresa's money right there."

And she stood there pointing to where some money lay, right there for everybody to see. I heard gasps from the other children, and I stood there feeling confused and bewildered, for I could not explain why there was money in my box when I was holding mine firmly in the palm of my hand. Lizzie stood there with a satisfied and triumphant look upon her face.

I desperately tried again to plead my innocence and explain that the money in my locker was not mine, but it all fell on deaf ears. I had been branded a thief and there was absolutely nothing that I could do about it. The teacher did not even want to know my side of the story, she didn't want to listen or to even ask me how come there was money in my box. She certainly didn't want to investigate the matter properly.

Instead, she continued to scold me and lectured me on what a bad little girl I was, as the children looked on with horrified and disbelieving looks upon their faces at this dreadful and evil thing that I had done to one of their classmates. And I have to say how I felt all alone as this teacher interrogated and humiliated me further in front of the whole class — scolding me, harshly telling me that I was a horrible child and nothing but a thief.

And, as I stood there red faced, shaking and feeling completely distraught, desperately willing myself not to cry, she leaned forward, lowering her face close to my own. The words she said next would traumatise me for many years to come.

"YOU HAD BETTER BEWARE, BECAUSE NO MATTER WHERE YOU ARE, I WILL ALWAYS BE WATCHING YOU."

I can't recall of how I got through the rest of that day; I felt like I had been condemned. Lizzie sat in the classroom with a rather pleased and smug look upon her face, while I sat waiting for the day to end so that I could go home with Mum.

I never mentioned about the ordeal of being accused of stealing, even though it had upset me terribly and had left me with an awful feeling of dread which was, to me, soul destroying. Even though my parents would have believed me, I just couldn't bring myself to tell them, and I suspect that was due to feeling ashamed that I had been accused of doing something so terrible. If she had known, Mum would have gone into school and had it out with the teacher, for none of her children were thieves. But, as it was, Mum never found out and I continued to live in fear of that horrible and rather vindictive teacher for many years after that particularly nasty incident. I even developed a fear that I would see her while with my family, shopping or on a day out. Her threatening words continued to haunt me as they kept repeating in my ears.

A few years later, long after I had left that school, I can remember accompanying my mum as we picked up my younger sister from school, and as we walked through the gate and into the playground, of suddenly being hit by such a strong feeling of dread that I instantly felt sick. I began to struggle to breathe and my whole body seemed to shake, I so desperately wanted to run and hide. Mum must have seen my sudden discomfort and asked if I was feeling alright, and I told her that I wasn't feeling very well, while my eyes frantically scanned the school building, afraid that she was lurking there watching me. I held tightly onto the side of the pushchair where my baby brother lay sleeping, shaking with fear and anxiety that I was feeling.

Looking back now I wish I had told my parents because that awful teacher had made my life a complete misery, and not only had I been condemned by her and been branded a thief, but she had given me a bad name, which also made it look bad on my parents. This made me angry, and she made me feel ashamed, and I hated her for it and I will never forgive her for what she did to me and how it affected my life, even to this day.

Even today I find it quite chilling and find it hard to comprehend how someone so young could have been so vindictive and devious as Lizzie in what she did to me. And if I was to think that going up to junior school was going to be much better, well - I was wrong.

CHAPTER EIGHTEEN
RIVERMEAD JUNIOR SCHOOL

After my harrowing experience during my time at Sunnymead Infant School, it was not long, before I found myself attending another local school. The Rivermead Junior School, which was situated down the high street, (along Walton Road) in West Molesey.

It was a fair walk from our home, and as Mum had my younger siblings to take care of, and my older sisters were at another school, I used to walk to school with Mrs Woods' daughter Claire.

I started a new class, a mixture of new faces and old faces from my previous class and school, including Lizzie Dawson. And although my teachers at this school were also quite strict, they were never nasty, mean, and they didn't discriminate against me.

Although I would sometimes join in and playing games with the other girls during the playtimes, I would often just simply wander aimlessly around, feeling lonely and bored. And this often left me a target for the bullies, certain older girls who took great pleasure in tormenting me. Soon I was left feeling anxious and nervous all the time, which led to my reluctance to attend school.

I would try anything possible to get out of going to school, especially on a Monday morning, which was always the worse for me. I would wake up, get myself out of bed, and then wander down to the kitchen where Mum was busily preparing breakfast for us all. I would tell her that I was feeling rather unwell, and she would look concerned and ask me what the matter with me was. I would then make out, as I usually did, that I was feeling very sick or that I had a tummy ache or something else – my list of ailments grew longer and longer – any excuse to keep me from going to school.

On occasion, Mum would take me to see our doctor, Dr Stuart whose surgery was situated, I believe, at his home down along Wolsey Road. This was a wide, tree lined road in East Molesey with huge, impressive houses with big windows and tall roofs. It was a fair walking distance from where we lived, and Mum's best friend, Frances Woods, who lived across from us, would often accompany us on our walk down to the doctors with us.

One morning, after having yet again complained of feeling unwell, Mum decided it was best to take me back down to see the doctor again. And, as usual, Mrs Woods accompanied us on the walk to his surgery.

Now I was incredibly happy about this, not just because I would be getting a day off school, but because, sometimes when returning home, we would go down Walton Road and pop into Woolworths just for a little look around. On the rare occasion, just for the very odd treat, they would stop off at the bakery to buy a couple of iced buns to have with their morning cup of tea and chat. And if that happened, I would be given half an iced bun to eat as well with them.

So, on this particular day, I was feeling quite happy with myself, as I would probably be told by the doctor that I should stay home for the next day or two, as that what Dr Stuart always recommended.

On the way down to the surgery, as we walked down those long roads with the large private houses, Mum and Mrs Woods stopped in front of a very big house with a rather large garden, which was surrounded by a waist-high brick wall where a large lavender bush sprouted wildly, bees swarming and buzzing around it. Now Mum loved the smell of lavender and she and Mrs Woods paused to put their noses near it and take in the fragrant aroma. They both brushed their hands through the bush and rubbed their fingers gently up and down over the purple flowery stems, admiring the sweet scent which filled the spring air with sweetness. Mum, feeling very naughty herself, pulled a sprig of it off the bush before we continued to make our way to the surgery.

Unfortunately, if I thought that things were going to work out well, I was wrong. Dr Stuart was usually a pleasant and happy man, but that day he was not. When Mum and I were called into his consulting room and Mum explained to him my symptoms the doctor asked me how I was feeling and then started examining me. He didn't seem particularly happy and he turned to Mum.

"There is absolutely nothing wrong with Theresa," he said to my utter dismay, and he went on to tell her that I would have been absolutely alright to have gone to school.

I can tell you that Mum was not too pleased with me for lying to her. It had been a long walk down to his surgery and, with the doctor being very abrupt and rather stern with her, she was obviously not happy. As we walked out of his consulting room, I was feeling rather dejected. That had not turned out well at all.

Once we made the long and solemn walk back home, Mum made sure that I got a good talking too for making out to her that I was ill and, although she was pleased that I had nothing wrong with me, made sure I understood that I had wasted her time. But then Mum, being soft, and being such a good Mum, still made sure that I had half of her iced bun.

CHAPTER NINETEEN
MY VISIT TO THE HEADMASTER

As my parents continued to have problems getting me to go to school, and as they had become increasingly concerned at how withdrawn I had become, they decided to go and see the head teacher of the school, Mr Dracus.

I can remember of Mum and Dad escorting me to school as I hadn't wanted to go, and as we reached the top of our road, I very quickly turned and shot of back towards home. Poor Mum, who had my younger baby brother in the pram, stood watching on helplessly as Dad ran up the road after me. Needless to say, when Dad caught up with me, he held on to me until we got to the school.

I also attended the meeting, sitting quietly in the head teacher's office as the adults discussed my concerns and troubles, including the reasons as to why I was so reluctant to come into school.

Afterwards Mr Dracus turned to me and smiled reassuringly, and as he knew how very shy and timid I was, he asked me various questions on my likes and dislikes at school and what lessons I enjoyed, as well as if I had friends and was I being picked on. I answered him the best that I could, open and honestly nodding my head in answer to his questions.

"Ok Theresa," he said as he leaned towards me, "if you get any more trouble at playtime and someone is really upsetting you, you come right along and see me and I will sort this problem out for you. So when you come to school from now on, you will have nothing to be afraid of, ok?"

I looked at him nervously, and nodded my head, meaning yes.

Mum and Dad were happy and satisfied when I told him that I would go to see him, and this gave them, as well as me, some encouragement and peace of mind. And, for a while, it did give me some hope and assurance while going to school, and it was especially nice and encouraging to have someone in authority that I could go to if things really did get bad for me.

I started going to school each day feeling a lot better, a lot more confident at leaving the safety of my home, and steadily my reluctance to go to school started to ease. But then my enthusiasm and the trust that I had for the head teacher quickly went flying out of the window.

Unfortunately, the bullying did not stop, and that put a strain on my confidence, although I did my best to ignore it. But a few weeks later, after that meeting with my parents and Mr Dracus, I was confronted by a group of older girls in the playground, who mercilessly tormented and shoved me around, making some very unkind and upsetting remarks as they did so. I stood there feeling embarrassed as they swarmed around me and – as the coward that I am – I remained frozen to the spot suffering their torments until they got bored with me. Finally, they went away laughing happily amongst themselves, and probably looking for some other poor soul who they could pick on.

As I watched them disappear, I suddenly remembered what Mr Dracus had told me. So, I decided to do the right thing and report the confrontation. I headed into the school building and made my way in the direction of his office.

I nervously and very gingerly walked up to his office and tapped on his door. I listened and he called out a couple of times for me to come on in, before I apprehensively opened the door and I took a couple of steps inside.

Mr Dracus was standing over his desk looking at some papers, and he turned and looked at me, quite surprised at first, and then he frowned.

"What do you want Theresa?" he asked abruptly. I quickly and quietly told him of what had just happened to me in the playground, including the name calling (I just didn't want to leave that part out.)

When I had finished, I waited for him to tell me that everything would be alright, and that he would certainly deal with the matter.

But no. Sadly, for me, that was not going to be the case.

He looked at me with exasperation on his face, and told me in what seemed to me in a most unpleasant manner, "Oh Theresa, do go outside and play, and do stop telling tales."

I stood there rather stunned for a second. This was a huge blow for me, for someone who had taken a lot of courage to go and see him.

I had expected words of encouragement from him. I was confused as was it not him who had told me that I was to go and see him if I was having any trouble and being picked on, and that I should go and see him at any time?

I felt my face go red and tears stung my eyes. I turned and made a hasty retreat out of his office and practically ran down the corridor, anything to get away from that embarrassing moment in his office.

I was feeling rather wretched. His comments made me feel small and worthless. I felt quite hurt and mortified. All I wanted to do right then was to go home.

I learnt a lesson that day. I would not tell anybody about my problems ever again, because to do so only brought me more pain and distress. He had intimidated me, and from that moment I had lost my faith in humanity. I would no longer trust an adult from outside of my family. Yet again I had been snubbed by an adult from the school that I was attending.

*

Reluctantly I continued to go to school, and although first play wasn't too bad, lunchtimes were a nightmare and I just continually walked around on my own, being unable to participate in the games that the other girls were playing.

The bullies often preyed upon me during those lonesome times, and the worst thing that happened to me during lunchtime was when a group of five girls locked me in the toilets — that incident, in time, had a massive effect upon my life.

It was a big mistake on my part and, truly, one of the worst things that I could ever have done, but being chased by a group of older girls – pursuing me like a pack of hunters after their prey around the playground for what seemed like forever – I really did not think clearly.

Hurrying into the nearest toilet cubical, I swung the door shut behind me. I spent a little while in the cubical while I tried to catch my breath and steady my pounding heart. I listened with my ear to the door, hoping that I had lost them, that they had got bored with me and would leave me alone.

I did not hear anything at first so; when I thought the coast was clear, I slowly and cautiously pushed open the door to go out. But suddenly the door was forcefully slammed shut from the other side, only just missing hitting me full in the face. For a split-second it took me completely by surprise, and I wondered what on earth was going on.

Puzzled, I knelt against the door and shoved as hard as I could, and, again for a split-second, it looked as if the door was going to open. Then it suddenly slammed shut once again. My heart went into my mouth as I realized that the reason the door would not open was because the bullies were holding it closed, stopping me from getting out.

I was trapped.

I felt a surge of panic hit me as I started to feel claustrophobic; the sides of the cubical seemed to close in all around me. With my heart pounding, I struggled against the door, shoving and pushing with all my might, desperately wanting to get out.

There was no one around who was going to help me so I started to plead for them to let me out, but my distress just amused them even more. So out of sheer frustration and immense fear I started banging on the door, completely desperate now to get out — my heart was hammering in my chest and I started to panic, desperately pleading with them again to let me out.

I heard them whispering to each other and then they started to laugh as they mocked me, imitating my cries for them to let me out. By now I was a nervous wreck and absolutely terrified, trapped and completely alone. And as I stood there completely exhausted, I knew I had no choice but to wait it out.

After what seemed like an eternity, I heard the school bell go, the ringing drifting across the playground and building, bringing lunchtime to a close. I put my ear to the door, and to my immense relieve I heard the girls' voices fading as they left the toilets, maybe disappointed that their entertainment had come to an end.

I cautiously opened the door ajar and peered out, relieved to find that they weren't there, waiting to pounce on me when I came out. I sighed with relieve and quickly hurried out and ran as fast as I could across the now empty playground and across to the school building, where I shot down the corridor, still feeling shaky from my experience, and into the safety of my classroom.

When I arrived home after school, I never mentioned to my parents of my ordeal that day. And, although, that incident had a drastic effect on my life, I remained silent about it. Just being back at home with my parents and family was all that mattered. After all, it was the only place that I always truly felt safe.

Unfortunately for me the bullying still continued, and it didn't just occur whilst I was at school, but outside too. As I was soon to find out.

CHAPTER TWENTY
FRIENDSHIP AND BERAYAL

The only friend that I ever had when I was at school was a girl named Claire Woods, and she was the only other person outside of my family that I could talk too with confidence and without being shy.

Our mums were great friends and, as we lived opposite, we saw each other often and I felt that I could really be myself with her. Our mums thought that it would be a good idea if Claire and I walked to school together. While I had been attending Sunnymead, Mum used to take me as I was far too young to go on my own, and as I was a shy child, she thought that it would be nice for us to walk to school together. Mrs Woods agreed, so, each morning I would walk to school with Claire, and by doing so we became really good friends. It felt good having a friend that I could always talk too.

We would meet early in the mornings at one or the other's house then we would walk to school chatting and laughing together as we went, sharing jokes and telling secrets to each other. Claire and I would always often have some amusing incident, or something that would happen that we found to be incredibly funny.

We would walk up Spreighton Road and then we would go up to the crossing, where there would always be a police officer who would stop traffic so the school children could cross Walton Road safely. On one particular morning there was a WPC who was helping people across the road. When the time came for Claire and I to cross, the officer strolled out to the middle of the road and held up her hands to stop the flow of traffic. On her command, Claire and I started to cross and, as I neared the middle of the road, I absentmindedly let a sweet wrapper drop onto the road. The policewoman looked at me and said in quite a serious tone, "Oh, you litter bug."

I felt so embarrassed I didn't know what to do with myself and I think I hung my head in shame. I can remember that my face turned bright red I quickly hurried over to the other side of the road and I really did feel bad over dropping litter on the ground. In fact, I felt so bad and ashamed with myself that I never dropped any rubbish onto the ground again. But once Clair and I had crossed and walked a little way up the road, we turned to each other and simply burst into fits of laughter.

Another incident while walking to school was on a horrible grey day when it had rained heavily during the night and the roads and pavements were glossy with rain. We had been chattering away together when suddenly a car which was coming towards us drove through a large puddle of water. The heavy spray of cold, dirty water shot straight over us soaking us from head to foot — we were drenched. We stopped walking and looked at each other — and burst out laughing. We may have been drenched, but like the troopers we were, we still continued on our way to school.

Time went on and as I began to face troubles at school, Clare's group of friends steadily expanded and, soon, Lizzie Dawson joined the crowd.

At first, during playtimes, we would play on our own or with a few other girls with whom I got on alright with, and we would all enjoy playing games like two balls, where each of us took turns to bounce two balls in various rhythms backwards and forwards onto the wall. Or we often played hopscotch, cat's cradle, or skipping with our skipping ropes. I can vaguely remember that sometimes we would also play with the beanie bags which the school had, but not all that often.

So, I do not know – or simply cannot understand – or begin to explain how things changed or, even why. I cannot even explain when it started, except that, gradually, Claire started to change and began to show a different side to her, one that I didn't know existed. And, pretty soon everything changed, leaving my life in turmoil. I cannot believe how one individual can suddenly change in such a manner that they can inflict and cause harm upon another. But that is what happened and what Claire did to me. She turned on me in the cruellest of ways, causing me distress and utter misery, all because she and her cruel friends wanted some fun and Claire wanted to show that she could be just like them. And I unfortunately became an easy target and victim for them.

Mornings were not so bad, but during home time after school, things started to change. Claire's friends started to accompany us on our walks home and I was soon made to feel unwelcomed as I strolled behind them as they huddled and bonded with each other. And, steadily, they started to show the nastiness they hid so well in the presence of adults, and which I got to find out about more frequently whilst coming home from school with them.

It had all suddenly changed one day, when a group of us were walking home from school. We were in a rather quiet and isolated area. Claire and her friends were walking ahead of me whispering and giggling amongst themselves. I don't know why, but I began to feel slightly uneasy, then suddenly I was taken completely by surprise as Claire and the others swarmed around me, enclosing me in a tight circle. I stood there helplessly as they started to shove me to and from between each other, then spinning me around until I was dizzy.

I tried to get away from them, staggering as I tried to escape from my tormentors, pleading for them to stop as they continued to taunt and threaten me — but Claire and one of the other girls stopped me. She roughly grabbed hold of my arms, forcing them down by my sides and telling me that under no circumstances was I to move. And, as I stood there, I had to endure their taunts and threats about what would happen to me if I moved. I stood and listened in fright as they threatened to leave me completely on my own — I was warned about what would happen If I was to disobey them, and I felt such a coward and really angry at myself for allowing them to continue tormenting me that dreadful day, and I hated them for it.

"Please stop! Just stop!" I begged them, feeling utterly distressed and humiliated at how they were treating me. And., I closed my eyes, just willing for this horrible nightmare to end wondering what I had done to have deserved it — I was literally at their mercy.

I opened my eyes and begged then once again before my emotions broke. I had just had enough of their bullying behaviour, and I fell to my knees on the ground and sobbed uncontrollably, utterly heartbroken and completely distraught. Claire came over and she put her arms around me.

"Oh Theresa, we were only having fun," she said trying not to laugh, obviously feeling triumphant at the control that she and the other girls had over me. She continued saying that they hadn't meant to scare me or to be mean, and the others started pretending to be sorry and sympathetic, all apologetic but looking thoroughly pleased with themselves.

We walked on home, me feeling all shaken up and on wobbly legs listened to them making up more excuses.

"It was a game, that's all."

"We never meant to upset you."

I knew they were buttering me up, that they were feeling fearful of me telling someone bout the bullying and getting them all into trouble. They had the nerve, pathetically, to ask me not to tell anyone about what they'd done, saying that it would never happen again. How I detested them for what they did to me, and I was so glad when I arrived home.

I never told Mum about what had happened that day, after all, it didn't seem fair to burden her with my problems. My parents sometimes had problems of their own, and I did not wish to trouble them further. So, when Mum asked me if I was alright, I just smiled at her and told her that I was. I never told her what I had allowed myself to be subjected to by Claire and her friends, their threatening behaviour and the anguish they had put me through.

After all, I had to learn to fight my own battles, to face up to my own responsibilities and fears

CHAPTER TWENTY-ONE
CLAIRE'S REVENGE

I wish that I could tell you that after that horrendous incident things slowly improved between Claire and myself and that, like the good friend she pretended to be, she reverted back to like how she used to be. But sadly, that was not the case.

Claire, almost unwillingly, continued to walk with me to and from school and, usually, it would be just the two of us. One day we were walking home when we noticed a cat in one of the gardens that looked exactly like my cat, Rum. A few months before Rum had ventured out like he usually did, but he never returned home. Despite searches, Rum had sadly disappeared.

We stopped by the wall that bordered the front garden of the house and the cat jumped up onto the wall. I stroked and made a fuss of him and he started purring.

"That is your cat." Claire said, looking at me. "That is your missing cat, Theresa."

"No, this isn't Rum," I replied shaking my head. Although the cat had very similar markings on him, I could tell that he was not Rum.

Claire suddenly reached out and grabbed the cat and held it firmly in her arms. He struggled to get down, but Claire held onto him tightly.

"Theresa, it is you missing cat. Come on, we will take it home with us."

"No, it definitely is not my cat," I told her once again. "You had better put it back on the wall. You can't just take him; he belongs to someone else".

But she refused and I started to feel very uncomfortable as she began to walk away.

"Leave the cat, Claire. Come on! Let's go home," I pleaded, but she stubbornly refused. I looked around me, anxiously wondering what to do, and it was then that I noticed a lady was watching us from the window of the house.

And it was then I became agitated with her.

"Put the cat down," I very sternly told her. Claire turned to me and I saw that she was not happy, so, I gently took the cat from out of her arms and placed it back onto the wall. I watched contentedly as it jumped down and very quickly ran towards the house, where it disappeared around the side. I felt satisfied, but Claire looked at me with annoyance.

"You have no right to yell at me," she complained as we started walking for home, and I explained to her that someone had been watching from the window and, if she had started walking up the road with the cat, then we would have been in a lot of trouble. Claire sighed and agreed that I was right, and she was glad that I had seen someone was watching us. We made our way home talking and exchanging gossips and about schoolwork. And when we got to our homes and parted ways, she seemed happy.

I too had felt incredibly pleased; I had stood my ground with Claire over the cat and, by doing so, had begun to feel a lot more confident in myself. From now on I would stand up for what was right and nothing was going to make me feel vulnerable again.

Or so I thought.

I spent the rest of that afternoon chatting with my sisters, reading books and having a nice conversation with Mum. She, as always, had cooked us a lovely dinner and afterwards I sat at the table reading my comics while Mum was working in the kitchen preparing food for when Dad came home from work.

It was then that there was a loud bang on the front door, and Mum went to investigate. I heard Mrs Woods talking to Mum as they came into the living room. Mum looked slightly puzzled as to what was going on, but Mrs Woods looked absolutely livid — she was fuming. She looked first at me and then turned to Mum, then back at me.

"Claire does not want to go to school with Theresa anymore," Mrs Woods said, staring crossly at where I sat.

Mum seemed surprised.

"Oh, has something happened then?"

Mrs Woods looked at me with such glaring eyes that my heart went into my mouth; I knew straight away what this was about, and my legs turned to jelly. My sisters who were also in the living room with me had gone deadly quiet. We had never seen Mrs Woods so angry before.

Claire came home from school very upset today," she said, turning to Mum, her voice full of anger. "Theresa had been very nasty and horrible to her, she was picking on her after school, so she doesn't want to walk there with her anymore."

I sat there stunned. Now that wasn't what had happened, that was not true at all.

"I didn't," I protested, shaking my head, looking across at Mum. "I wasn't mean to her!"

Mum looked at me concerned.

"I am sure Theresa wouldn't have been nasty to Claire," she said to her friend, who looked as if she was going in for the kill.

"Claire said she was!" Mrs Woods scowled, turning once again to look at me. "She said you were! So she doesn't want to walk with you anymore."

So, just like the teachers had been before, Mrs Woods was not at all bothered to ask for my side of the story. And the accusation made against me in my own home proved too much. Instead of standing up for myself and saying that it was not what had happened and telling my side of the story, I did what I usually did in such situations and burst into tears.

Mum hurried over and gently put her arm around me to comfort me as I sobbed, and just like that, Mrs Woods changed her tone of voice and become concerned.

"Don't worry Theresa, don't get upset. I will talk to Claire, and she will still go to school with you, ok?"

She had the nerve to smile at me. First, she had been so hostile she had frightened the life out of me, and now she was acting all sympathetically. I wasn't in floods of tears because of her, and I couldn't really care less if I went to school with her daughter or not. What I was hurt about the most was Claire — because of all that she had put me through; the bullying, her threats and all the mocking and taunting I had had to endure from her and her spiteful friends, about which I had never once told Mum about.

And even today, when I had saved her from getting into trouble by stopping her from taking the lady's cat, Claire still felt the need to make false accusations against me. She had lied to her mum about what had happened, and all because she hadn't liked it that I had been firm with her and had stuck up for myself.

She had betrayed me and all because she wanted revenge.

Mum saw Mrs Woods out. Afterwards Jenny turned to her. "Goodness Mum, did you see her face? It was like thunder."

Mum frowned. I don't think she was very happy – not because of me – but because of Mrs Woods for coming in and being so aggressive towards me.

I continued walking to school with Claire, but from then on things were never the same between us. In fact, I cannot understand why she did what she did to me. Not only had she betrayed me, but worse was that she humiliated me in front of my family, my mum and my siblings. Instead of being thankful towards me for what I had done, she had branded me a bully and I would never forgive her for that.

CHAPTER TWENTY-TWO
REPERCUSSIONS AND A LESSON TAUGHT

Looking back now, I cannot fully explain – nor could I ever truly understand – my reasons for having remained quiet and never telling Mum about the horrors, the abuse, the lies, and all the bullying that had been inflicted upon me while I was attending school.

I can only think or (assume) that the reason why, at the time, was that maybe a part of me was scared of upsetting her. So I had chosen to remain quite over the following years and kept all of my sufferings and all my pent-up emotions to myself.

And looking back upon my life now, I can remember an incident when I did reveal to Mum something that had happened. It was the one and only time I spoke out about something that had been said to me, and which, to my horror, would leave Mum feeling devastated.

Thinking back now all these years later to that particular day, I did wonder at first, after seeing her shocked reaction, if maybe sometimes it is best to remain quiet. But, true to my mum's nature, after I had told her she stood up for her family. And I realise now how important her words of wisdom, advice, and her dignity were, and how they went on to teach me a very valuable and important lesson.

On the day in question we had been invited to our aunt's house for an afternoon tea. Mum revealed to us that we had all been invited, and although I cannot remember what occasion that afternoon tea was for, at the time I probably didn't care. I was doing something different from my usual routine — I was going to meet Mum and my other siblings there after school. I believe my dad met us there as well, after he had finished work. I was quite so excited about it that I just couldn't wait.

As one of my aunt's daughters also attended the same school as I did, it was suggested by my mum and aunt that my cousin, Leanne, and I would be walking home to Leanne and my aunt's house. So, Leanne and I made arrangements the day before about where we should meet up after school, and on that day, I went to school quite happily, looking forward to meeting Mum at my aunt's, and also walking to her home with Leanne. It was a very rare occasion for us to be doing something different, especially during a weekday, so I was full of excitement and just could not wait for when school finished.

Lessons that day seemed to drag on and on and I spent my time daydreaming and watching the large clock on the wall. When, finally, the bell went and I was finally allowed to go, I hurriedly got my coat from its peg, and hastily left the cloakroom. I hurried to the place where Leanne and I had arranged to meet, (at the end of the school building opposite the entrance of the school gate), shouldering my way through the mass of children. I was the first one there, so I dropped my bag by my feet and waited for my cousin.

I watched as the other children hurriedly left the school building in droves, some giggling and some larking about in small groups as they headed across the playground and out through the gates. I waited for a while, watching as the playground emptied and fell more silent.

Then I became suddenly aware that I was completely on my own, and felt quite abandoned waiting there. I started to feel slightly anxious. I decided to wait just a while longer, but still there was no sign of Leanne.

"Where is she?"

I became increasingly concerned.

Had I come to the wrong meeting place?

No. This was where we did agree to meet.

I decided to go and look for her.

I left our arranged meeting spot and ventured nervously back towards the school. And as I came towards the side of the building, I heard voices. I peered around the side and saw Leanne in deep conversations with her friends. Absentmindedly, I called out to her and waved. They all turned my way and Leanne gave me a quick smile.

"Wait there, I won't be a minute," she called over before turning back to her friends, and I watched as the girls started whispering in hushed voices, obviously not wanting me to hear what they were saying to each other.

I stood where I was and waited and Leanne would look around at me every now and then and I was aware that they were talking about me, and I stood there feeling rather embarrassed and anxious to be getting going.

After what seemed like a lifetime Leanne finally moved away from her friends and walked over. Her friends stood watching, whispering in hushed voices and giggling. I noticed that Leanne looked rather nervous, and looked at me rather sheepishly as she approached.

She spoke to me in a very quiet voice.

"Look Theresa," She said, indicating towards her friends as she did so, "if they come up to you tomorrow and ask you why we are walking home together, and that you are coming around to my place, can you just tell them that we are good friends and that our families know each other. They don't need to know that we are all related or anything."

I must admit she had left me lost for words and I just stood there stunned at what she had just said to me. But Leanne just continued on with her disgusting charade, thinking that I was a complete idiot. There was no way that I would tell them that we were not related.

"It would be far better for people to think of us as friends than us being related," she carried on as we started to walk away from her watchful friends and in the direction of the gate, smiling at me with that sweet false smile of hers.

I did not answer her back — I just couldn't. I was completely shocked and outraged by her snide and disgusting comments. I could not believe what I was hearing, that in other words what she really meant was that she was ashamed and embarrassed to be seen with me because I and my family were from a working-class background. And that meant that she would be ashamed of her friends knowing she was related to my mum and dad. She was stuck up and a snob, and she was embarrassed and horrified at her friends finding out that she and her family were related to us.

At first, I felt very uncomfortable, and then I became disgusted with her. To me her comments were an offensive and unacceptable attitude to have.

As we walked to her home I felt completely gutted, and her comments left me thinking them over in my mind. It was nice being around my aunt and uncle's house, and my aunt greeted me warmly like she always did, and it had been nice seeing Mum there, having a laugh as she and my aunt chatted to each other while they had their tea and us children played. But that spark of excitement that I had faded, and watching my mum, my aunt my siblings and cousins, I felt an overwhelming sense of immense guilt, that I had not stood up for myself, and worse still I had not stood up for my parents. My parents may not have been financially well-off, but that had not meant they had shown us all less love and respect, and they had still provided for me and my siblings and had always been there for me in times of trouble — they truly were the best parents that anyone could wish to have.

But Leanne's words hung over me like a black cloud, what a nerve she had to snub us, and to run down me and my family like that. It made me to feel very angry, and I was tormented by the fact that I had not said anything to her and defended my family. I simply lost all respect of her then. And although I had always kept things to myself, for the first time in my life I did what I thought was right, I revealed to Mum what Leanne had said to me, though I hadn't quite expected the reaction that I was about to get after I had confided in her.

CHAPTER TWENTY-THREE
MUM'S ANGUISH

Although life in my family had its up and downs, my parents having the occasional row sometimes, or my siblings and I having fights and arguments with each other, there was one thing I knew that Mum always took pride in, and that was us.

Mum took a lot of pride in how she and Dad bought up my siblings and myself, and if there was something that Mum hated more than anything – and of which upset her considerably – it was people being snobbish towards her or us.

Mum had once confided in me about a time when she worked in an office. She disliked working there and found it very uncomfortable, and when I had asked her why she replied that it was because the girls who worked there were very snobbish and would always look down their noses at her. And Mum absolutely hated that. She felt that nobody should be judged on the way they looked or how they lived, or if they were wealthy or poor.

But if things ever had an effect on Mum, she never showed it. So, I was not prepared for Mum's reaction when I finally told her of what Leanne had said to me a few days earlier. I had pondered for days on whether or not I should say something, and if so, how. It had bothered me an awful lot and it still played on my mind relentlessly, and I did feel rather bad that I had not stuck up for myself or for my parents. So in the end my conscience got the better of me, and I approached Mum, when she was in the kitchen busily preparing lunch.

Mum patiently listened as we sat at the table where I told her what Leanne had said to me, going into as many details as I could. I told her about having to wait for her for what seemed like an age and how she never showed up, and then the comments she had then made to me.

Afterwards Mum was very quiet for a second, registering in her mind what I had just told her, and I began to feel a little uncomfortable and began to wonder if perhaps I should have just left things be. The last thing that I wanted to do was to cause trouble for Mum, but my loyalty to her and Dad was important to me.

But Mum's reaction was not what I had expected at all.

To say that Mum was cross was an understatement. Mum was gutted and extremely hurt at what I had just told her.

"How dare she say that?" Mum said rather bitterly. I had never seen her so angry and, to my concern, she became very upset. "Who on earth does she think she is? Looking down her nose at us like that! And not wanting her friends to know that she is related to us!"

Mum became very worked up and seeing her in that state made me feel upset too. But Leanne had wronged us.

"Just because they own their own house and their own car. And just because her dad has a good well-paid job and they can afford to go away on holidays abroad and have the luxuries that we don't have does not mean that they are better than us," Mum cried. "We are just as good as them! What right as she got to run us down, and to be ashamed of being related to us?"

As I listened, I felt terrible at how upset she had become, and I suddenly felt wretched, and for a second, I regretted saying anything to her — the last thing that I had wanted to do was to cause Mum unnecessary hurt. I felt terribly sorry for her and completely dreadful.

But Mum suddenly stopped and she looked at me with concern etched upon her face. What she said next was her words of wisdom to me that I have never forgotten. "Theresa don't you ever let anybody run you down or look down their nose at you." Very seriously she said to me, "You always hold your head up high, and never be ashamed of who you are, or where you come from."

She smiled at me then and, as I sat there in front of her, I felt a great sense of love and pride for her, and I felt privileged and so lucky that she was my mum.

I never knew if Mum ever said anything to my aunt and uncle, or whether my parents said anything to Leanne, following my confession. She never came up and apologized or spoke to me much after that. Life just went on and continued as normal for us, but her shameful words to me that day, which hurt Mum considerably and caused her such distress, are something which I have never forgotten.

I went on through life, always respecting my parents and how they had brought me up.

CHAPTER TWENTY-FOUR
MY EXCITING DAY AT THE FUNFAIR, WITH A
SIXPENCE TO SPEND

I, like many other kids, looked forward to Easter; and that weekend, while my sisters and myself got excited as we wondered how many eggs we would be receiving, Mum went about the house, busily doing her usual household chores making sure that the house was polished, neat and tidy. Then every Good Friday I would get up to the lovely smell of hot cross buns warming up in the oven. My aunts and uncles would pay us a visit as they did every year, to drop off the eggs that they had bought for us, and they would have a cup of tea and a chat with my parents, before either heading on home or going to pay another relative a visit.

But it wasn't just the Easter holidays or the receiving of our chocolate eggs which I found to be exciting; it was our yearly trip to the funfair which I always looked forward to. With the coming of spring, came the daffodils and the blossoms on the trees. There would be slight warmth in the air, and later, during April or May, the ground would be basked in sunlight and the delightful sight of the bluebells. Then the funfair came down to Hampton Court and pitched up on the green at Bushy Park, and during the bank holiday weekends families would flock there for the entertainment and enjoyment that it bought.

On the day that we usually went – mostly I believe was Saturdays – we would, after having had our lunch, wait until Dad came home from the pub so that, he too, could eat. Then we would all set out. My mum would always make sure that we were washed, neat and tidy before we went out.

To me it was an exciting and unforgettable day out, being amongst the swarming crowds; the rock and roll music blaring so loud that you could hear it far down the road even before you had arrived. The atmosphere you felt as you walked amidst the stalls and entertainments was completely exhilarating; and then there was that special feeling you get as you are captivated by the noise of the people who have gathered there, and of the activities that are going on around you.

There's the thrill of trying to win a prize playing on the roll a penny, or maybe having a go at trying to get a ball into a bowl so you could win a goldfish. Then there was the candy floss and toffee apple stalls, and as you continued walking around came the strong smell of hotdogs and burgers cooking.

But then, best of all, there were the rides. So many rides were scattered around on the field. Adult rides like the twister that went around ever so fast, weaving in and out, as it did. There were the bumper cars, the ghost train which, if I ever did get to ride on, I spent the entire time with my eyes covered. And not forgetting the huge, enormous Ferris wheel, which peered over the treetops high above all the other attractions. And there are the children's rides that went around nice and slow, small cars or aeroplanes which children could ride cheerfully with glee.

But the best ride of all, the one which I loved going on more than anything, was the merry-go-round. The circular ride with those magnificent horses and the twisted brass pole that lifted and lowered the galloping steeds whenever the ride was in motion, going round and round.

I would stand eagerly waiting for the ride to stop so that I could be helped up onto a horse. Then Mum would tell me to hold on tight, and there was that funny feeling that you get as you wait for the ride to start. And when it does start to go around, it's just pure joy.

Oh, how I loved sitting there upon my horse, that wondrous feeling as your horse goes up and down, round and round, the breeze upon your face, watching the people as they disappear in a quick blur as you whizz pass them. The sheer feeling of euphoria broken only when your ride slowly comes to a stop and you then, very reluctantly, have to get off. It was perfect, I just did not want it to end, and to me, it was truly a unforgettable experience.

Mum and Dad always gave each of us a sixpence to spend and would allow each of us a ride and a go at trying to win a prize. I can remember one year of actually winning a goldfish and quite happily carrying it home with me. I called him Goldie and I kept him for quite some time.

I can't remember if Dad ever went on any of the rides, but Mum made sure she had her fun too. She loved the Whistler, a ride that whizzed around really fast, going in and out as it did so. It was one of the rides that I can remember my mum going on every time we went to the fair. And for some reason I hated her going on that ride as I felt afraid for her, and so I was always so glad, and rather relieved when it eventually stopped and Mum was able to get off. And she would always come of that ride full of laughter and looking really happy. The atmosphere was always great and I always had so much fun that I just wanted that day at the funfair to last forever.

I always had a fantastic time, and always looked forward to another year when I would be able to go to the funfair with my family. We might only be able to go on these trips once a year, but that didn't matter, because trips out with my parents were rather special, and something that I hold very dear to my heart.

But eventually things come to an end, and before you knew it, I, along with my family, would rather reluctantly, make our way home from the funfair.

We would walk following the main road which led across Hampton Court Bridge and through East Molesey, but we would not go straight home, as when we reached Molesey, my parents and relatives would always stop off at the New Inn pub for a drink.

The New Inn was a towering block of a pub sitting on a wide corner of Walton and Matheson roads close by to St Mary's church. It was a bit of an adventure for me, and quite exciting as, while the adults were in the pub, my sisters and I would remain outside and amuse ourselves, and to us it was a treat. We never messed around or played in the road, we just literally chased each other up and down the pavement, or discussed topics of interest, talking excitedly amongst ourselves about the afternoon we had just spent at the fair.

My dad would come out with a bottle of coke with a straw and a packet of crisps for each of us. During the Sixties children were not allowed into pubs, they were for adults only. But I can remember of one incident one year when, whilst outside, the weather suddenly changed and it became rather stormy and, as we stood there, we could hear the rumbles of thunder rolling in the distance. As the storm gradually got nearer and the thunder louder and the sky turned black Mum became worried about us. The landlord and landlady knew my dad rather well, so my sisters and I were ushered in through the bar and put into one of their private rooms. To us children that was rather exciting.

When the adults had finished and stepped out, we would set off again and we would stop of at the chippy and buy a chip supper. Often my relatives would all stop of at our house to have a meal with us before heading on back to their home. One particular bank holiday weekend though, my trip with my family to the funfair will be something that I will certainly never forget.

Mum as usual had made sure that my sisters and I were dressed smartly and ready to go out. She had painstakingly brushed and then plaited my hair, before tying the braids, as she often did, in bright coloured ribbons. I had put on my favourite best dress along with a pale coloured cardigan, short white socks and – I believe – red sandals. My parents had given us a sixpence each to spend at the funfair, and I had put mine carefully into my small white purse. My sisters and I then waited eagerly and impatiently for Dad to come home from the pub so that he could have his dinner and then we would be able to finally go on our way.

How I can remember those long waits we had to endure and how time seemed to go on forever before Dad finally came home, letting himself in and we would then sit around the table, watching his every mouthful, silently willing for him to hurry up. But, even when he had finished his lunch, he would then have to quickly go and check the racing results before going into the bathroom to get himself ready. I can remember those anxious waits so well, it all seemed endless. And as if feeling our own torment, Mum would give Dad a good talking too for taking so long, and would tell him to hurry up because we had all been waiting for ages and that it wasn't fair. And all the while my siblings and I would still be pacing the floor, anxiously waiting for him to get ready.

And when Dad was finished and ready to leave, and we had finally made our way out of the house, we would all cheer and get very excited. We always met up with our relatives, Aunt Edith, and Uncle Bob and their son Simon, who accompanied us to the fairground.

The walk into Hampton Court was quite a long one, and when you are very young it seemed to last forever. One road always to me seemed particularly long, but the thrill of the fair would will me on. I was captivated by the sights of the village I was born in as we made our way into Hampton Court. In the distance I was always intrigued by the church steeple that I could see towering up over the rooftops, and as we neared closer and closer to our destination, I could see the rounded top of the Ferris wheel and the sounds of the music reached my ears.

I cannot begin to describe the atmosphere and of the wondrous feeling that I felt as we neared Hampton court green; to me it was one of sheer delight, the noises of the music and of the people was deafening, and the excitement showed on the faces of the other young children who were tightly clinging on to their mother's hands.

I watched fascinated as a man tried selling balloons to the people who were busily hurrying by, all eager to reach the fairground. I saw the many policemen that were walking amongst the crowds as they went about their duty, making sure that the traffic flowed, and everything was in order — also helping anyone who needed their assistance and making sure everyone stayed safe.

We had only just arrived at the funfair, and we had started to take a slow walk across the green and I was dawdling behind Mum and Dad and the rest of the family, minding my own business and taking in the spectacular sight before me. I was feeling excited and elated as I held my white purse with my sixpence in it, walking along oblivious to what was going on around me, when suddenly, from out of nowhere, a man suddenly approached me. He told me to stand still and quickly, before I could react, he shoved a small monkey into my arms.

I was absolutely dumbfounded. I had never seen a real-life monkey before, let alone held one. The man shoved my arms around its small body, and the little monkey, who was dressed in tiny long-sleeved jumper and trousers, suddenly clutched onto my arm. I felt ecstatic and could not believe that I was holding on to this little defenceless monkey. I thought he was so small and soft, cute and absolutely adorable. But I can also remember, at the time, being frightened and absolutely terrified that I might accidently squash him.

The man got in front of me told me to stand very still; he had a camera focused on me. And I can remember feeling, at that moment, being very important. But I was soon jolted back into reality when Mum came over to see why I had stopped and looked surprised when she saw the photographer taking shots of me holding the monkey. She was not at all pleased.

The photographer suddenly grabbed the monkey away from me, which I was very disappointed by. I really wanted to take him home with me. I watched as Mum chatted to the chap, and she looked over at me before turning back and paid him some money.

When Mum got hold of my hand and walked me away, she smiled at me and asked why I had let him give me the monkey to hold. "You should not have allowed him to take your picture Theresa," she said, as she now reluctantly had to pay him.

I felt slightly guilty because Mum could not really afford to pay for a photo, but she knew how chuffed I was and I told her that he had taken me completely by surprise. Mum smiled and said, "Well, they are going to post the picture to me, I just hope that the picture turns out alright."

But when Mum did eventually receive the photo, she was very disappointed and not too happy.

"Oh, look — they haven't even got all her feet in," Mum cried, exasperated.

But to me that did not matter. I loved the photo, and I still have it to this day. I will certainly never forget the day that I had held that cute little monkey in my arms. He had felt so soft that I would love to have kept him. I was the envy of my siblings that day, and I just couldn't stop talking or thinking about him.

Going to the funfair was always a very special time for me. I always had great fun, and it was always a day out. But for me, it was the day I held and had my photo taken with a monkey that was most marvellous to me. The most special and wonderful experience of my life, and one which I will never ever forget.

CHAPTER TWENTY-FIVE
IMAGINARY GAMES AND SUMMER PICNICS

At last, the summer holidays have began. Schools were now closed and ahead were weeks of freedom and fun; so away went my winter wear and out would come my summer clothes consisting of my summer dresses, cardigans (in case the weather was to get slightly chilly), my short socks and my sandals.

The sun would shine gloriously and the birds would be singing way up high in the trees and upon the rooftops. There would be the sounds of children shouting and laughing as they played in their back gardens in the neighbourhood, there would be the sweet fragrant aromas of the different varieties of flowers that grew around the borders in our back garden. There would be butterflies of brilliant colours flitting and fluttering among the flowers and, from all around the garden, you could hear the loud humming of the bumble bees as they were attracted to the lavender bush.

My sisters and I spent many happy days during the summer playing together out in our back garden. Mum never allowed us to play out in the street and I can remember her saying to us, "You have a nice back garden to play in, you don't need to play out in the road."

I truly believe that Mum just felt happier knowing where we were and that we were safe, and I didn't mind one bit — to me it was great. We would simply play for hours in our back garden, and we were always finding different things to do to keep us occupied.

My sisters and I would sit crossed-legged on the grass, making daisy chains and seeing who could make the longest chain, chatting away as we did so. Or sometimes, we would pick buttercups and hold them under each other's chins, to see if our chins turned yellow, and getting excited if they did.

Although we never went away on holidays, my sisters and I would still enjoy ourselves. We played games and we had fun and – on most days throughout the summer holidays – we would, after we had got bored with either doing puzzles, colouring in books, or reading our comics, go outside into the garden to play where we would amuse ourselves using our imaginations to inventing games to play.

It was one of these particular occasions during a hot summer that I can remember extremely well and which hold special memories for me. Jenny, Pearl and I had decided to play at being pirates and our parents had allowed us to use an old wooden table that they were going to get rid of. It was a square table which was made of solid wood and which had rather thick solid legs. It was extremely heavy, but, between the three of us we soon managed to carry it safely down into the bottom of the garden, where we placed it carefully onto the ground with the legs facing upwards.

We sighed with relief and smiled as we looked down at the table; we were happy and completely satisfied, as we finally had our pirate ship. We placed a pirate flag, which we had made that morning, onto one of the legs, and then we made ourselves pirate hats out of old newspaper, which we placed upon our heads.

We were pirates and we simply let our imagination run away with us. We allowed ourselves to believe we were sailing across a raging sea, seeking for lost treasure, and we placed obstacles around the garden to be our steppingstones. They led from our ship and across the garden to a wide area near the back door which was to be our treasure island.

Each of us would try to cross the stones without falling off, and if one of us did we would have landed in the sea. I can vaguely remember that we had fun by making each other walk the plank. There was lots of laughter and we had such a jolly good time.

On one other occasion, whilst my sisters and I were playing outside, I had asked Mum if I could make a wig-wham or tent, and whether or not she had something that I could use to make one with. Mum told me she would see what she could do for me and, a little while later, she came out into the garden carrying an old sheet. Mum even helped me to make the tent, and although I am unable to remember now as to what Mum used to make the base with, I can remember of how grand it had looked. My sisters and I simply loved crawling through the opening of our tent and sitting inside there. I can even remember the time Mum brought me a glass of orange juice and some biscuits; I felt so important. To me it was my secret sanctuary, and I thought it really was rather grand. And it's one memory that I will always cherish and will never forget.

On the odd occasion, when I was very little, Mum would stop whatever she was doing and come outside into the back garden to join in our games. I can recall one time fondly when she did this when we had played what's the time Mr Wolf? A fun chasing came when you would approach whoever the wolf was from behind and ask the time before they would say "Dinner Time" and proceed to chase you. It was very exciting and a lot more fun with Mum standing there being the wolf, while my sisters and I would try to silently creep up behind her, and then running off squealing with laughter as she suddenly turned around to try and catch us. I had so much fun that evening, and having Mum join in with us it really did make it even the more special.

But our summer holidays weren't just spent at home; as Mum made sure that we had a treat by going on daytrips out. And one thing we especially looked forward to was a picnic at the park.

My aunt Betty and her children always accompanied us on these events, when we often went to either Bushy Park or to the local rec — the green field along Walton Road in Molesey. We would all sit on the grass and Mum and my aunt would place a blanket down on the ground then lay out the food. We would all eat chattering and laughing at each other and then, afterwards, Mum would let us all run around and play. There was a children's playground at the rec and I loved the swing — you could sit there and just keep going higher and higher until you felt like you could reach the sky. Oh, how I loved that funny feeling you would get in your stomach as you went backwards and forwards on the swing. It was just great.

Most times we would have a picnic at Cigarette Island which was in Hampton Court. (Cigarette Island was once a small patch of land that was surrounded by three stretches of rivers: the Amber, the Mole and the Thames. The Hampton Court railway station was located on the Island, and the only access to and from the station was by going over a narrow bridge. The station had coal sheds or bunkers and stored plenty of coal. The Island itself was actually named after a houseboat, Cigarette, that was moored there in the 1920s. In the early 1930s. the river Mole was filled in for the new bridge at Hampton Court, and in 1935 Cigarette Island was opened to the public as a municipal park.) To me it seemed a rather large park, which had a very tall metal slide. I can remember my sisters and I having lots of fun there.

Often, we enjoyed feeding the ducks, either at Cigarette Island or at Bushy Park. Mum was very fond of swans and she once told me that she thought they were rather beautiful birds and looked quite proud with their long thin necks. We could have spent absolutely hours feeding the cavorting ducks and those graceful swans.

We always used to walk there, sometimes walking along the river, or along the road, and we always enjoyed the picnics, having a jolly good time. There was one picnic that we had there that I will never forget; an incident which I had found to be very frightening, and which could have had severe consequences. That one time what my sisters and I witnessed on our fun day out could so easily have ended in tragedy.

It started as a normal day. With our picnic food prepared – Mum had seen to it that I and my other siblings were looking presentable and ready for going out – and we all waited impatiently for my aunt and cousins to arrive so that we could be on our way. I was feeling very excited as I loved going out in the fresh air and feeling the sun on my face, getting away from the house for a while with Mum, which also gave her a break from doing the housework. It was a time for her to relax and enjoy herself as well.

When our relatives finally arrived, we set of on our walk down to Hampton Court; I don't remember much of my journey there or of coming home because I was quite young. But I know that when we arrived Mum and my aunt put down a blanket for us all to sit around, then they laid out our food; sandwiches, fruit, and then – as a special treat – some cake. There was orange squash for us to drink.

I can remember running around playing happily with my sisters and cousins and going playing on the swings and even on the high slide, though only once or twice as I was not very keen on it.

It was quite a pleasant day, and there were a few other families also out having picnics and enjoying themselves, and the afternoon was great that I didn't want it to end. I went back to where Mum sat chatting away with my aunt, and Mum gave me some more squash and asked me if I was enjoying myself, and I told her that I was, before running off to play with my sisters and cousins once again.

After a lot of running around I began to walk towards the river; it was very wide and I had been told it was quite deep, and as I had a fear of water I stood well away from the edge. My sisters soon joined me, and we walked along by the riverbank where branches and foliage overhung the water's edge.

I stopped walking and watched and marvelled at the many dragonflies that hovered silently over the surface of the water before flying off again. I stopping every now and then if there was something interesting to see like a fish in the water or a duck — our cousins joined up with us and we laughed and gossiped together.

As I looked out towards, to the other side of the water, scanning the horizon for some particular bird that I might see, I suddenly heard a great splash from my right, followed by a loud yell — and then a child's voice cried out.

For a split second I froze, I just knew that some child was in trouble and there, in the middle of the river, was a small boy struggling with all his might trying to keep afloat, to stop going under, but to no avail. The more he struggled the more desperate he became, and I was petrified that this small boy was going to drown. I had never felt so helpless in all my life.

People gathered around and someone started yelling for the boy to hang on as he struggled to stay afloat. I ran off to fetch Mum and she and my aunt came running to see if they could help, but by then a woman had waded into the water and with a long branch in her hands reached across as far as she could and got the boy to grab hold of the end, and managed to pull him out of the water.

I was so relieved that he was saved, and the poor boy stood there shivering, I expect more from the shock of nearly drowning than the cold. My sister told us that the woman who got him out had told her afterwards that she was looking after the boy that day for a friend, and I have often wondered of how the friend had felt about her son nearly drowning on that hot summer's day.

We packed up shortly afterwards and went home. Although we had all enjoyed ourselves, and we had all had a lot of fun, for me that was one of the most frightening things I have ever experienced — although the boy was saved that incident could have ended so tragically. For a long time afterwards, I couldn't stop thinking about that young lad who nearly drowned. It certainly was a picnic that I will never forget.

CHAPTER TWENTY-SIX
A FAMILY DAY TRIP TO THE SEASIDE

Although, as a child, we were unable to go away for holidays, that did not mean our summers were spent restricted to our home. Every year Mum and Dad would always make sure that at least once a year we went on a day trip to the seaside. I believe the trip was organised through Dad's local pub, and my aunts and uncles and other relations went along too, so it was quite a family affair. It was something that I really looked forward to as it was one of those rare special moments where we were all able to go out for the day as a family.

On the morning of our departure, whilst my sisters and I went around the house, eagerly waiting for when it would be time to leave, Mum would be checking that she had everything ready to take with us before we left the house. She would have boiled eggs the night before, and then packed them that morning, along with sandwiches, fruit and squashes.

I can remember the excitement I felt as we left the house on a Sunday morning with the sun shining down on me as I walked alongside Mum and Dad to where the coach was waiting. And then that sheer joy I felt as we finally boarded the coach and took a seat and set off on our journey to the seaside.

To any child the coach trip seemed very long, and to me it seemed to go on forever. I was not a very good traveller and always felt sick, even when I first set foot on the coach; there was always that strong smell that turned my stomach, so I could never wait to be able to get off.

I can remember once Mum had asked my uncle, Bob, if he would mind giving me one of the sickness pills that he had given his son before the coach departed. So Uncle Bob took one of the pills out and placed it in the palm of his hand for me to take.

Now, I was a very stubborn child and I refused to take the pill – after all, I didn't know what it would do to me – so I refused. And, no matter how much coaxing there was from Mum or my uncle, they just could not persuade me to take that pill. My uncle even went as far as demonstrating to me how safe it was, by popping one into his own mouth, but to no avail.

Mum told me not unkindly, that I wasn't to moan if I felt sick as I should have taken the pill, it would have stopped me from feeling sick and I would enjoy the journey a little better. And on that particular outing I can remember feeling really sick, but no way was I going to let Mum and my uncle know that, I thought it was rather wise to just keep quiet.

Halfway through the journey, the couch would pull in and stop for a while so the driver and his passengers could stretch their legs, use the toilets and to have a drink. Us children would run around and play together, enjoying a moment of freedom from sitting on a stuffy coach, before, once again, boarding for the last part of our journey. I remember one year when a cousin of my dad's kindly handed out tubes of smarties to each of us children as we stepped off the coach.

I can remember of the thrill I felt, as from the coach window, I saw the outline of the coast in the distance. Then when we finally arrived at our destination, I eagerly made my way off the coach, relieved to be breathing in some fresh sea air and hearing the cries of the seagulls as they flew low along the promenade scavenging for food.

Mum and Dad made sure that we were all together before heading off towards the beach. I, along with my sisters, all felt very excited, especially as we made our way onto the beach. I would notice that there were a few families already there, with the adults all seated on deckchairs chatting away amongst each other as their children sat building sandcastles.

While my parents busied themselves getting decking chairs for themselves, my sisters and I wasted no time; we eagerly and hurriedly took our socks and shoes off and ran along to the water's edge, the sand soft and warm under my feet. I watched as the waves rushed in towards me and I gingerly dipped my toes into the sea and squealed with delight, as well as slight feelings of apprehension as the waves rushed over my feet numbing them a little. We all ran back to and fro, trying to get away from the waves, and then we would cautiously go back again, half in excitement and half in fear.

I would hear my dad anxiously telling my mum to keep an eye on us as we were getting too near the water and that it was dangerous. Then I would hear Mum telling him that we were ok, we were just having fun and that we were perfectly safe, and that she was there watching us.

"They're too close to the water, Vi," he would say. Poor Dad had a terrible fear of water, so he hated us children being so near the sea. Unfortunately, I too grew up to have a dreadful fear of water, so I have never learned to swim.

I happily spent my time playing in the sand with my bucket and spade, which I had bought along with me, relishing the freedom at being outdoors, my sisters and I chatting happily amongst ourselves as we made sandcastles. I could feel the sun and the spray from the sea on my face, and it was to me a very tranquil time.

We all had our lunch on the beach, with Mum and my Aunt Edith and I can remember eating my eggs and sandwiches, kneeling on the sand next to Mum, enjoying the glorious moment. The men, I think, would have had gone for a quick pint before returning later to have their sandwiches.

Sometimes, after our food, we would all walk around the shops, marvelling at the marvellous things that were displayed in the windows of the shops. My sisters and I always went into a shop to buy a stick of rock to take home with us. After all, how can you go to the seaside for the day and not take home a stick of rock? No, I don't think that would be right.

It was always a great day out, and I had so much fun, but before long and much to our dismay we all had to pack up and head back to the coach so that we could go home.

I can remember one year when it had been a beautifully hot day and I had had so much fun, that I actually – after having asked Mum, for what must have been the hundredth time, "Are we nearly home yet?" – fell asleep during the journey home. And suddenly I was being awoken by one of Dad's relations, telling me that we were back home now, and that I had to get off the coach.

After Mum and Dad had unlocked the front door and let us in, feeling rather bleary eyed as I made my way up to bed, I turned to them and I told them that I had a great time, and that I thought it had been a truly wonderful day.

I just could not wait to go back to the seaside again.

CHAPTER TWENTY-SEVEN
THOSE DREADED WINTER MONTHS

As the summer gradually turned towards winter and the autumn leaves started to fall from the trees, leaving them looking desolate and bare – as the warm evenings grew cooler – Mum and Dad would prepare for when they had to light the coal fire, making sure that they had enough coal to keep us warm and snug during those cold dark winter days ahead.

Dad himself would then make sure that the chimney was clear of soot, and that the hearth was ready for lighting. He would use a chimney brush with a very long pole handle, which was attached to the end of another pole, and then another, until it was long enough to be able to reach far up into the chimney pot. If the chimney was not cleared of soot, it could catch fire, or cause a lot of smoke. Then we would have to call in the chimneysweep — it was said to be very lucky if you shook their hand, and especially fortunate for a bride and groom if a chimneysweep was to wish them good luck on their wedding day.

Coal was delivered once a week and the coalman would carry a huge sack of coal on his shoulders, through to the garden, and then would carefully let the coal fall from the sack into the coalbunker. It was a very dirty and dusty job, but necessary for people to keep warm. Once all was done and the weather was cold enough for the fire to be needed, it would soon fill our living room with warmth from the fire, making it cosy and warm.

Oh, how I absolutely hated the winter months; the cold and damp mornings, the wind and the rain lashing against the windowpanes, or how the wind and rain battered at your face as I ventured to or from school, or out shopping with Mum. And the dark, bleak evenings, which made everything seem gloomy and rather desolate. The two things that I looked forward to during the bleak winter was Bonfire Night then Christmas.

Those winter days and nights were thoroughly depressing, and the winter seemed to go on forever. I hated the cold and the rain, when everything around seemed dismal and rather bleak. I would spend the evenings sitting with Mum and Dad in the living room watching the television in the comfort of the fire that blazed in the hearth, spreading its warmth around the room, and making everything nice and cosy.

And how I hated having to go to bed at night, moving away from the warmth of the living room where the flames from the fire burning brightly, giving the room a calm relaxed feeling. Going out into the chilly hallway to make my way, slowly and gingerly, up the stairs to the top of the landing — while the light from below would always cast eerie, sinister shadows upon the wall. Once I had made my way into my bedroom I would, as I always did every night, look behind the door and under my bed.

That was a thing I did for many years, growing up with an awful fear of something hiding under there; a sinister spectre just waiting to pounce and cause me harm as soon as I was in bed and the light was turned out, plunging the room into darkness. I would peep out across to my bedroom windows, dreading and fearing the night and of what lurked outside — the unknown.

We had no heating in those days apart from the fire in the living room, so the bedrooms were bitterly cold in the winter. Our bedding consisted of sheets, a couple of blankets and a bedspread. I always draped my coat over my bed, which was something I did for many, many years to come.

I hated having to get myself undressed and I would do it as quickly as I could so that I could put on my nightdress and then quickly clamber into bed. It is hard to describe how cold it was at first, lying there between sheets that felt just as cold as the bedroom itself. But after a while, I would start to feel warm, and I would snuggle down into the bedclothes, and fall asleep, knowing that Mum would leave the light on in the landing for me, so that if I woke up during the night I would not awake in the dark.

In the mornings there would be, during most of the winter, ice on the inside of the windowpane. And it would be so bitterly cold that, as soon as I got out of the bed in the mornings, I would rush to get myself washed and dressed before running downstairs to the living room, where I would sit in front of the nice cosy fire that Dad had already lit. Then I would get myself warmed up before going into the kitchen, where Mum would be preparing a nice bowl of porridge for my breakfast. It was something that we all definitely needed on those cold and sometimes frosty winter mornings.

Another thing that we had to endure occasionally was smog — a combination of fog and smoke. Sometimes, from the warming fires burning away in the houses, a thick smoke would billow up into the frosty skies. If this smoke combined with fog, it could suddenly descend upon us so thickly you couldn't see in front of you. It was very dirty due to the coal, and breathing it in was extremely bad for your health. It was a very unpleasant occurrence, and people walking outside would often cover their mouths with scarves to keep from breathing the dreadful smog in.

Children, coming out of school and being collected by their mums, would all run in different directions, calling out to each other as they did so, trying to find each other. To them it was great fun. But for me, it was a frightening experience, an absolute nightmare.

I can remember one day when the smog was quite thick. Mum came to collect my sisters and I from school. Mum told us to stay with her but, as she spoke to another parent, my sisters and some other children ran off into the smog to see if they could all find each other. Now, I was a bit of a chicken and was intending to remain close by Mum's side, but for a split second I made the decision to follow my sister, after all, what harm would it do?

But how wrong I was!

I couldn't find my sisters and, worse still, soon I didn't know which direction I had come from and didn't know where to go to find my way back to Mum. I stood there surrounded by a thick, yellowy-white blanket of nothingness and it felt so strange — I could not see my hand in front of my face. It was eerie and nerve-racking. I tried to listen and, for a second, I felt panic hit me. From all around there was nothingness, silent and still and isolating, and I began to feel disorientated and my heart started beating faster. I listened, hoping to hear the sound of one of my sisters, but it was completely quiet and the smog overpowering. I suddenly began to feel alone and very vulnerable.

And then, with intense relief, I heard Mum's voice calling out for me to come back to her. I quickly went in the direction of her voice and thankfully I finally managed to find my way back to her; it was such a relieve that I remained close by her all the way during our walk back home.

Going to school on bitterly cold mornings was a nightmare, especially if it was frosty — although I wore long socks, by the time I arrived at school my legs would be frozen. And it was even worse during lunchtime break, when I would spend my time just walking around the playground trying to keep myself warm.

But whenever Halloween drew near, I was able to join the other kids in the playground, because I was fascinated by the stories they told; there was always talk about ghosts and witches, especially about Baba Yaga, the Scandinavian hag of folklore who enjoyed feasting on the bones of children. I listened intrigued in the cold playground as the others told stories of Baba Yaga, who would come out on her broomstick every Halloween night at midnight and rap on your bedroom window.

It was very exciting and I couldn't wait for Halloween to come. Halloween was not celebrated like it is today, but we had our stories and our games. I can remember one Halloween when I had come home from school all excited and anxious about Baba Yaga who would be doing her rounds that very night and choosing someone's window to rap on. Mum had made us our dinner and after we had finished and washed and cleared away everything, she got a bowl of water with some apples in for each of us to try to bob. It was great fun as we took turns in trying to get an apple from the bowl using only our mouths. But as I have said before, I was really quiet the scaredy cat, and once it was bedtime and I was tucked up in my bed, I literally lay there terrified. I did my best trying to not look out toward the window just in case Baba Yaga was there peering in at me. She would be flying through the sky on her broomstick, and what if she should choose to stop off at our house?

I would know, as suddenly, through the quite of the night, you would hear that dreaded sound as she tapped upon your window.

TAP… TAP… TAP

Thankfully, sleep would claim me, and I would wake the following morning on the first of November, safe for yet another year. And with the arrival of November came the celebration of Guy Fawkes Night – or Bonfire Night – when families would light bonfires in their back gardens and fireworks raced across the night sky in dazzling colours.

I never particularly liked fireworks, well not being outside when my dad went outside and lit them, but I did love looking at them from the safety of my window. (Well, I did tell you that I was a wimp, or a scaredy cat, more like.)

We, like many other families, liked to follow the old traditions of Bonfire Night, which tell the story of Guy Fawkes' failed attempt to blow up the Houses of Parliament back in the 1600s. It was customary to make a scarecrow (a Guy, as named after the infamous culprit) and to light bonfires and to set off fireworks every 5th November – the night Guy Fawkes' plot was exposed by the authorities. There was always great excitement and many children would make a guy and then stand outside a shop, or somewhere where there were people passing by, and try and get some money for fireworks.

"Penny for the guy?" they would ask passers-by while proudly displaying their scarecrows.

Now one day leading up to Bonfire Night, my sisters and I decided to make a guy ourselves. Dad had some old shirts and trousers that he didn't want anymore, and Mum gave us an old sack with which to make the torso. I think we used a stuffed pillowcase for the head. I do remember that we worked pretty hard and well as we went about making him human, and in the end, we had our own guy.

I cannot remember now of whether we got many pennies for him, but we did enjoy showing him off and wheeling him around in either a wheelbarrow or pram. And it was certainly a lot of fun.

On the actual night Dad lit the bonfire it was great; the flames flickered, casting an eerie glow around the quite dark garden. All the neighbours along the street had lit their bonfires too, and the smoke from them cast a hazy atmosphere in the air.

Mum and Dad told us to bring our guy out so that we could put it on the fire, and then Dad would light the fireworks.

Now for me the problem was that I did not want to put my guy onto the bonfire. In a silly way I hated burning it — not after all of the hard work we had put into creating him. But I had no choice, and stupid as I am I did not feel comfortable seeing my dad throwing the figure onto the bonfire and watching as it perished amongst the flames. I felt absolutely dreadful, and terribly guilty – it was not like it was a real living being – but I absolutely hated it and I certainly never made a guy ever again after that.

When my sisters and I finally went to bed later that evening we watched from our bedroom windows all the bonfires which were still aglow in the neighbouring gardens. And then I would watch and marvel at the spectacular sights of fireworks lighting up the sky.

It was superb and a truly amazing sight to see.

CHAPTER TWENTY-EIGHT
A VERY MAGICAL CHRISTMAS

The most wonderful and exciting time of the year for me was Christmas. I loved the atmosphere leading up to that big and exciting day, the festivities that went on around you as the grownups went about their Christmas shopping, or the fun and euphoria I felt as Mum and Dad put a tree up in the living room, where the pine needles would sometimes drop onto the floor and the room would always be cosy with the crackling of the fire and the smell of the tree. It always filled me with the thrill of the Advent season, which made the winter seem a lot less dreary and a lot more magical.

The build-up in my day was exciting and simply wonderful. Christmas, back then, was not commercialised like it is today. So, leading up to Christmas then was a lot different, as we children learnt to appreciate what we had and what we got and we were thankful for that one present that we received. And whatever you got on Christmas morning it meant a lot.

Another thing that I can remember is, nearing Christmas Eve, how jolly and polite people were towards you. Everyone seemed to be jovial and in the Christmas mood; many a time I would hear of someone shouting out "Merry Christmas" from across the road.

Then there was the fun of my sisters and I sitting at the table in the living room, busily making paper chains and seeing who could make the longest one. And then hearing the Christmas carols being sung outside, groups of children wandering the cold roads singing the festive songs. Mum's favourite was 'Silent Night' and even now, whenever I hear it, I always think of her and the magical Christmases she and Dad gave me.

I can remember one time – when I was slightly older – going around the houses with a few other girls doing Christmas carolling. Now that was great fun, although I found it to be nerve-racking, especially when the homeowners would open their front door and listen to you singing before they dropped either a three pence or a sixpence into the palm of your hand, and even more especially when one is as shy as I was, but I did it without running away.

Even going to school at that time of year became less tiresome and more enjoyable. I remember singing carols with the other children in the classroom as we celebrated the Christmas festivities. I can remember during my infant years at Sunnymead, sitting at my desk and colouring in a self-made Christmas card, which I would take home to my parents after school. When I had finished colouring in, I would write to Mummy and Daddy on the inside of the card followed by a little message. Then I would tenderly write my name and put a few kisses at the end. After that I would eagerly wait for the end of school when I would meet Mum outside so that I could hand my Christmas card over to her.

At school during that time of year there was also a surprise visit that we had from a very special visitor — Father Christmas! He would be dressed splendidly in his red suit with the white cuffs and his hat with a golden bell and with his white bushy beard upon his cheery face. I would be in awe of him as he came bursting into our classroom with the big sack of toys upon his back.

"HO HO HO," he bellowed that famous phrase of his. And I would sit nervously in my chair with my arms upon my desk, staring at this wondrous figure feeling excited and slightly apprehensive.

"I hope you children have all been good this year," he said happily to us all, and you could feel the excitement from everyone as he dropped himself down into the chair which had been provided, saying otherwise he would not be able to come down our chimneys and deliver presents to our houses. He really hoped that we had all been especially good for our mums and dads so that he would be able to deliver us some toys.

Then he would rummage around in his giant sack where the sound of gifts rattling could be heard and pull out a toy. He would call out each child's name and that child would go over to him and take a present and, as with all the other children in the classroom that afternoon, I eagerly waited for my name to be called.

And then there it was! My name! "Theresa Ayres," he called in that very loud, hearty voice of his. And do you think that I leapt up and eagerly went over to him, like all the other children in the classroom did?

No, you must be joking if you thought that!

I am ashamed to say that I completely let myself down. I was so frightened that I simply froze on the spot. I had turned completely and utterly shy, and was just too scared to move away from my desk. I sat there frozen to the spot and nervously looked across at him, to where he waited with a toy in his hand.

"Come on Theresa, it's alright," my teacher tried to coax me out of my chair and, at first, I refused to move. So, she got up and decided to come over with me. I walked over nervously to this great man on legs that felt very wobbly and took my gift from him, shyly whispering a quick thank you as I did so. I hurried back to my chair, holding on tight to my present and feeling so very, very glad that I had not lost out on it and had survived my encounter with Father Christmas.

*

As with any child I could never wait for Christmas Day to come, and those days on the calendar seemed to drag by so very slowly. But for me I found Christmas Eve was just as exciting as Christmas Day.

Whenever Christmas Eve came around I, along with my other siblings, would be full of excitement. We would all make sure, early that day, that we would have one of our socks ready for taking to bed with us that night, to lay neatly on the bottom of our bed.

As Dad did every morning, he had lit and made up the fire, warming the living room up and sending of a pleasant glow around the room, making me feel nice and snug, whilst outside the weather was bitterly cold.

Mum, as usual, would be busy tidying up the living room, making sure that it was all clean, polished and looking presentable. And then, afterwards, she would be busy working in the kitchen, where she would be preparing and cooking mince pies and homemade sausage rolls, which always smelt so good and appetizing.

Every Christmas, Mum and Dad always had a proper ham joint bought from the local butcher. I have no recollection of whether or not Mum had to cook or boil it the day before Christmas or whether it came already cooked.

On one particular Christmas Eve when I was 7 or 8 years old, Mum sent me across the road to buy some eggs from one of the neighbours that she knew well and who kept chickens. I can remember knocking on the door and the elderly neighbour asking me in. I stood there in her living room waiting as she went outside into her back garden to fetch some eggs. We talked when she came back in and started counting the dozen eggs into the carton; asking me if I was excited about Father Christmas coming that night, and of whether or not I had been a good girl for my mum.

I told her that I had been.

Ok, I told a little white lie, as I wasn't always good, but I wasn't a bad child either. I just played my parents up about going to school, that was all

The neighbour smiled at me as she handed over the eggs and I gave her the money. With bids of farewell and wishes of Merry Christmas, she held the door open for me and I ran back to my house, being very careful to not drop the eggs as I did so.

I can remember when I got home that they had a Christmassy film on about Rudolph the Red Nosed Reindeer, and I sat watching it with my sisters by the warming fire surrounded by the rich smell from the Christmas tree, which always added to the joy and excitement of the Christmas spirit.

During the afternoon Dad always bought home the Christmas turkey with him when he returned from the pub, and much to my dismay and that of my sisters, the fresh bird would still be whole. Dad carried it through from the kitchen and into the living room with its neck and legs still attached to it, dangling from his arms. We would all scream, running from him and he playfully made out that he was going to touch us with the turkey. Looking back, those moments bring a warm glow to me. They were such special moments in my life, and they are something I will never forget.

Now, as a child, I always hated going to bed when I was told to do so. But on this night, I couldn't wait for bedtime to come and, when it eventually arrived, I would carry my sock up to bed with me, where I would tenderly lay it onto the bottom of my bed. Once satisfied that Father Christmas would be able to see it, I quickly jumped under the covers and snuggled up in my bed, where Mum would come in and kiss me goodnight.

"You must go to sleep Theresa, otherwise Father Christmas will not come down the chimney and deliver any presents," Mum would say gently, and after she had left the room, I let my imagination run completely away with me; I really could believe that I could hear sleigh bells ringing.

"Did you hear that?" I called out to my sisters. "It's the sound of Father Christmas's bells! He's on his way! Oh, we had better fall asleep soon."

"Yes, I can too," one of my sisters cried out excitedly. All my sisters thought they had heard it and we all desperately willed ourselves to sleep.

And finally, I fell asleep dreaming of Christmas. And when I awoke the following morning, what a lovely surprise awaited us all.

CHAPTER TWENTY-NINE
A MAGICAL CHRISTMAS DAY

I awoke up early and full of excitement on Christmas morning, having dreamt the previous night of Christmas, and of what I might get from Father Christmas.

It was still a little dark outside and the bedroom felt cold. Before risking getting out of bed, I had wanted to make sure that Father Christmas had indeed been and had made his rounds at our house. So, beneath the warmth of my heavy covers, I gingerly straightened out my leg and lifted my foot slightly too where I had laid my sock the night before. I held my breath in anticipation as I poked with my foot and my heart leapt for joy as I felt the weight of the sock above my bed sheets.

I jumped up in my bed with a squeal of delight, stirring my sisters from their sleep as I yelled in excitement. "Father Christmas has been," I shouted out to my sisters, feeling grateful that he had not indeed passed our house.

I grabbed hold of my sock, which was heaving and bulging, and sat on the bottom of my bed. I peered inside and took out the contents of the sock one by one; there was a tangerine, an apple, a banana and a small bar of chocolate.

Mum came into the bedroom and greeted us all. We were eager to head downstairs, but Mum told us not to go down just yet, but to wait until Dad had lit the fire and warmed up the living room for us.

"Then you can all come downstairs to see what presents Father Christmas had left for us," Mum told us as we waited excitedly. Then she hurried down to where Dad was tendering to the fire. Eager to get my presents, I hurriedly got myself washed and dressed, and then my sisters and I patiently waited until it was warm enough for us to go downstairs.

When Mum finally called up to us that we could now come downstairs, we all shot down as fast as our legs could go, all of us eager and excited. The warmth from the living room was very comforting and inviting and gave the room a cosy feel.

I stared in both disbelief and in awe at the transformation of the room — it was truly magical. The sideboard which, only the night before had looked exactly like it did every day, was now spread with the treats of the seasonal period. A bowl of nuts of many different varieties – walnuts, chestnuts, monkey-nuts, Brazil nuts and almonds – and there was even a silver nutcracker laid beside it. There was a box of Turkish delight, a tin of Quality Street or, some other years, Cadbury Roses, and an oblong carton of figs, which always had a small strange looking wooden fork, along with a box of dates. And, finally, there was a large glass bowl of fruits: apples, oranges, satsumas, bananas and grapes and pears.

It was such a wonderous sight; the whole room had been transformed from when I had gone to bed the previous night, and being so very young and naive, I really believed that Father Christmas had done all this upon his arrival. It was simply amazing and to me, coming downstairs to this grand sight was simply magical.

I could not, back then, comprehend that it had been the hard work of my parents before they too had gone to bed, who had tenderly and carefully put all the extras to the room to make it all the more Christmassy for us. Not until years later did I learn to appreciate just what my parents did for my siblings and I every Christmas throughout our childhood. And looking back upon them days now, I see how much my mum and Dad did for us during the year, when they put money aside so that we could all share a good and memorable Christmas.

And then, best of all, there in the middle of the living room floor were our presents, which were stacked and full to the top in a large coal sack, ready and waiting for us.

As we all sat excitedly on the sofa my parents stood over the sack and, one by one, started to pull the presents out from the sack. They would read out the name on the label, and then hand over each present. Soon Christmas paper lay in tatters littering the floor as we ripped open our gifts, our bodies juddering with excitement.

I can still picture those special moments even now.

I have so much admiration for my parents. They would do their utmost to get us children whatever we wanted for Christmas, no matter how long or how much it took them to do it. Apart from the gift we received from our relatives, we only got the one present from our parents, but that was ok. We were always grateful for whatever we got from them. Us children meant so much to them that it was important to do whatever they could to get each of us what we wanted on Christmas morning. And that is exactly what they did for me one Christmas.

I can remember one year leading up to Christmas, Mum had asked me what I would like. I knew straight away, and couldn't wait to tell her. I wanted a doll, a doll that most of the girls at school had and was, at the time, very popular.

"I want a Beatle doll, Mum," I pleaded; I had wanted that doll really badly. The doll was not really called a Beatle doll, but was known and referred as one because of the thick, black hair it had on its head. I so desperately wanted one that, in my mind, I wished for nothing else.

So, on that Christmas morning, when Mum had been handing out the presents, my eyes widened with excitement as she then pulled an oblong box of the right size out of the sack and handed it to me. I knew exactly what it was! it was a doll; and I just could not contain my excitement.

But then Mum, looking rather worried and very concerned, said to me, "I am so sorry Theresa, I hope you won't be too disappointed, but your Dad and I were unable to get you the doll you really wanted." She told me this gently. "We went and searched everywhere for the doll you wanted, but unfortunately, we could not get one for you anywhere. But we saw this doll in the shop and bought you this one instead. I really hope you won't be too disappointed, and that you like the doll that we have got for you."

I looked at Mum with the concerned look of disappointment upon her face, but I did not feel angry or disappointed that they could not get me the Beatle doll. I soon learned from Mum that they had traipsed everywhere to try to get hold of my doll and, for me, that was all that mattered.

"Don't worry Mum, I'm sure I will simply love this doll," I reassured her. I hurriedly and eagerly unwrapped my present.

And there it was!

My Roddy doll may not have had the hair like the Beatle doll, but I fell in love with him straight away. As my doll had been bought with no clothes on, before wrapping him up, Mum had put one of my baby brother's vests on him.

I held my doll in my arms and looked at him with a mixture of amazement and pride; I was completely over the moon with him. I thanked Mum and Dad and kissed them both gratefully.

"He is the best doll that I had ever had," I told them, and I meant it. I carried my doll Roddy around with me all day; wherever I went, my doll would go to. My parent especially, my mum, were so relieved and happy that I liked my doll. It really meant a lot to her. How lucky was I to have such truly amazing and selfless parents like I did?

And I still have my Roddy doll even to this day.

The rest of the morning I spent playing with my toys, or with my siblings, showing each other the presents we had received. Then we watched the television while Mum prepared the dinner. Every Christmas morning they would show a programme where a television presenter would go around a children's hospital to the bedsides of different children, talk and laugh with them for a bit, and then hand over a Christmas present to them. Mum used to always come in to watch that programme; she used to find it very emotional. And even though I was young, I used to feel so sorry for the children that were in hospital away from their mums and dads and family, especially on Christmas Day.

For Christmas dinner Mum cooked for us a golden turkey, accompanied by her lovely roast potatoes and sprouts, followed by Christmas pudding or mince pies and custard. There would always be a sixpence in the pudding and it would bring good luck and fortune to whoever found it in their bowl. I remember the year that Pearl found it in her slice of pudding — I believe we had Christmas crackers which we all loved to pull.

After dinner we would enjoy a lazy afternoon playing with our toys until teatime, when Mum would put on a special spread of salad with her home cooked ham, Heinz salad cream and many jars of different pickles! Piccalilli, red cabbage, gherkins and pickled onions with plenty of vinegar, which my dad absolutely loved. And all this was followed by jelly and best of all, Mum's amazing trifle, which she had made the night before. Delicious.

Mum would always have a Christmas cake, but the one I mostly remember my parents getting was a Dundee cake; it was a fruit cake and the top was covered with sliced almonds. The spread that my parents put on for us every year was absolutely amazing and the food delicious.

And then after tea we would do something that was a tradition to the Ayres family, something we did every Christmas. And it is something that my older sister Jenny, still does to this very day.

CHAPTER THIRTY
A CHRISTMAS VISIT TO GRANDAD'S HOUSE

Every evening on Christmas Day, my parents would take us all down to Grandad's house. As I can remember, this happened for quite a few years, and we were not the only ones to visit him — all the family gathered there, my aunts and uncles and my cousins. It was quite a family tradition and it was something that was very important to my grandfather.

The house was small but that didn't matter, the evening would be filled with happiness and laughter, everyone feeling the joys of the Christmas spirit. The grown-ups would drink, talk and have a laugh amongst themselves, while us children mixed and mingled with our cousins, some that we very rarely saw, and probably only on the odd or special occasion.

Grandad loved having his family around him. He would always entertain us, and would always be dressed smart and sharp in a white shirt, waistcoat and black tie. It was crowded, and everyone was always welcomed. But there was still one other visitor to yet arrive.

The highlight of the evening was the grand and unexpected arrival of Father Christmas. It was very exciting and such a great surprise for all of us children. We would sit and gather excitedly, wide-eyed, faces beaming round our parents as Father Christmas bundled into the room.

"MERRY CHRISTMAS!" he bellowed, as he walked in through the door, and we all squealed with excitement, not just at the thought of who had arrived but also that he had a sack of presents perched upon his back.

The excitement intensified as Father Christmas hunched himself over his sack, and I watched him intently as he started to pick out various presents; I began to feel very nervous at the arrival of this great man.

"Jennifer," he bellowed as he pulled out a present.

"Simon."

"Pearl."

I watched as my siblings and my cousins went over to him and received their presents.

"Leanne."

And then my name was called out.

"Theresa."

But I didn't budge. Just like at school, I froze.

Father Christmas held the present out so that I could see it, a gift delicately wrapped up with Christmas wrapping paper. But, still, I could not move.

Father Christmas smiled and tried to coax me over to take the present from him, but I had gone all shy again. Some of my aunts laughed but not in an unkind way, they found it amusing, I suppose, as they knew how shy I was.

Mum and Dad tried softly to get me to go over to get my present from him, at first to no avail, but eventually Mum and Dad and my siblings managed to get me to go over to Father Christmas and to receive my gift.

And very quick I was indeed to take my present and hurry back to Mum. And everyone laughed and sighed with relief.

After handing out the presents, Father Christmas waved and bid everyone a Merry Christmas and left as quickly and as silently as he had arrived. I never knew or suspected the identity of Father Christmas who visited us every year on Christmas evening. It was Pearl who a few years later, during one of his visits, got rather suspicious and went from room to room seeing if any of our relatives were missing or not. Later she reported back her findings.

"It's Uncle Ken," she said. "He was the only person missing."

Afterwards Grandad would get his accordion out and entertain us all with his music as us children played with our new toys, sharing games and fun and laughter.

We would remain around my grandparent's house throughout the whole evening. I would have happily unwrapped my present, played with my sisters and we would have showed each other what we had got from Father Christmas, and then, before we knew it, Mum and Dad would be telling us that it was time to go home.

We would put on our coats and say cheerio to everyone, grownups hugging each other as they say their goodbyes, children being kissed or cuddled. When we had arrived back home Mum would get us to bed, where I would go to sleep dreaming of the wonderful Christmas I had had.

And, as always happens every year, Christmas had come to an end for yet another year. The day after Boxing Day things started to slowly go back to normal. Dad would go back to work that day, and I would start dreading going back to school. Although we probably saw in the New Year, we never really celebrated it. Back in those days, I can't remember many people celebrating it like they do these days. I can't remember any working person having the day off, as we do today. The New Year's Day didn't become a bank holiday until 1974. Rather, Mum would be making sure we had our clothes neatly ironed, and she still kept busy with the chores and as my dad, my brothers and sisters and I would be going back to school on the first day of a new year.

So, they were important for us all, those days after Christmas when we sat indoors around the crackling fireplace, while outside the cold late December wind howled around the houses and blew smoke from the chimney. Where, in the warming glow of the fire us kids sat together watching the television in the living room, and Mum and Dad, after having seen to the younger children and cradled their sleeping baby, sat in their chairs for a well-earned rest, Dad falling asleep with the newspaper in his lap, and Mum clicking away as she knitted.

These memories that I cherish will always remain with me forever.

EPILOGUE

When I now look back to those years when as a child, I remember how I used to sit in the classroom forever staring up at the clock on the wall, dismayed by how slowly the minutes were ticking by and wishing that they would just go so much more quickly. Never once did I understand just at how quickly time really does fly.

Minute after minute, hour after hour, day after day, year after year — time moves forward so quickly, just like a tide pulling you out to sea. Sadly, it does not stand still, and as it flows, you will find that special moments in your life get left behind. And, although they may no longer be there with you, you never forget certain aspects of your life, which linger in your memories as the years flow by.

I eventually moved on to senior school, and although still shy, I made a couple of new friends, who I got on with remarkably well and who made me feel more positive about myself. I will admit, I still struggled with my schooling during my senior years, but a good teacher, Mr. Smith, who I had an enormous crush on, helped me to overcome my fears and taught me the art of how to express myself whilst reading. Thanks to him I become a good reader who enjoyed and loved reading books, which encouraged the development of my self-confidence.

I remained at home living with my parents until in my early twenties, when I met and fell for a Hersham chap, Clive, who I courted and then married in November 1976.

I have now lived in my home in Molesey for over 35 years. I have been married to Clive for well over 40 years, and we have two amazing and loving children, a son and daughter, Adam and Sharon, and our two incredible grandchildren, James and Emily. All of whom I am immensely proud off.

Over the past 20 years or so I have suffered from a phobia, a fear of being alone, which has made me unable to go out anywhere on my own. I have to rely on and be accompanied by my husband, son or daughter, who have always been there for me, getting me out and about these past few years, visiting different places, and helping me regain my confidence.

But I am happy. In my spare time I have my crafts, I listen to music and I love to read books, and I can honestly say I enjoy my life.

I have a terrible fear of the dark – something which stems from my childhood – and I always have to carry a torch around with me during the evenings and at night. But I have no regrets, and feel I have been incredibly lucky. I have my wonderful family, and I am always accompanied by my loving Chihuahua, Gambit, who's a tremendous comfort to me, and who is forever and always by my side.

I may have my phobias and problems, but I feel strong and confident that I am no longer the shy person that I used to be. I am no longer afraid to stick up for myself; I will always fight for what I strongly believe in and in what I feel is right. This was especially true when I became a mother myself. Only in motherhood did I come to understand that I had a duty to protect my children, and to stand up and fight for what was right for them — just as Mum always did for us. I learned because I had the most amazing parents; that no matter what they were going through, they were always there for me; offering me advice and guidance, and helping me get through the bad times.

I learned a lot from my parents and, when, sadly, they passed away, it left a huge hole in my life. They truly were an inspiration to me, and without them I wouldn't have become the person that I am today. My parents taught me so many valuable lessons throughout my childhood and adult life. They taught me to be honest and to always be thankful for what was ever given to me, to appreciate in life what you have got, to never look down upon a person less fortunate than yourself. But, most importantly, to protect, cherish, love and respect your children, and to never be ashamed or forget where you come from.

And I most certainly never will.

I am proud of the lessons I learned from my parents, who faced greater hardships during their childhood than I did, but who still gave the best to their children. I am so very proud of who I am, and of my Romany, working class roots, and of growing up learning the true values of what family life and who you are is all about.

You don't need wealth or to have lots of money to enjoy the pleasures of life. I grew up with my parents and siblings in a three bedroomed council house in Spreighton Road in West Molesey in Surrey and I am very proud of it, and of who I am and of where I come from.

Mum's words of wisdom were always with me as I grew up, all through my youth and into my adulthood when I raised my own children. Her words are with me now when she said, "Theresa, never let anybody run you down or look down their nose at you. You stand tall, and hold your head up high, and never forget who or where you come from, because they are no better than us."

And Mum was right; no one is better than us, better than my parents and how they had brought us children up. No, they are no better than us; you see we were so very much, much better than them.

And Mum's words will always remain with me forever, as with those other memories that hold very special moments in my heart.

Those walks Mum and I took along the river. Going on picnics with her. Mum's smile and of her lovingly plaiting my hair and tying the braids with coloured ribbons.

Dad singing on a Sunday evening, and his special gift to me, when I was ill. Of us all singing along to the wireless before going to bed.

And of the special outings and many trips out that Mum and Dad provided for me and my brothers and sisters.

Summer days I spent playing outside in the back garden with my sisters. And our walks together down the road.

Grandad in his crisp white shirt and waistcoat, playing on his accordion.

Those special Christmases that they always gave us.

And the strong smell of lavender polish.

Mum once told me that she feared that when she was gone that she would be forgotten. She said that she hoped no one would ever forget her. I assured her that, there was no way that would ever happen.

They will live on forever in my memories and in my heart.

And this book is dedicated to them.

THE END

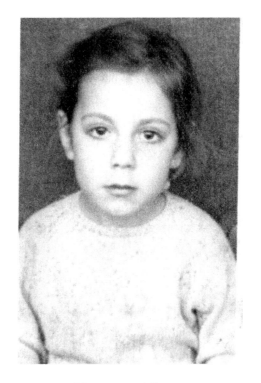

Me – aged 5

Mum & Dad holding a baby who could have
been either Jenny, Pearl or even me.

The photo of me holding the monkey at
Hampton Court Fair.

Dad in his army uniform (1940's)

Mum when she met dad.

My grandad Joseph Ayres with his daughter
Juney.

Spreighton Road during the 60's where I
spent my childhood.

A photo from the 1920's of Rivermead Junior
School.

With my dad at my wedding (1976)

My husband Clive and I with my mum and
dad. (1976)

TOP: Mum with her first granddaughter, Rachael.
LEFT: With mum holding my niece, Michelle.

Mum with my daughter Sharon.

TOP: Mum & Dad with Sharon
BELOW: Mum holding my son Adam.

TOP: Mum & I on a Sunday trip out with my children. (1980's)
RIGHT: Mum & Dad with their grandchildren, Sharon and Jason. (1980's)

OPPOSITE TOP: Clive & I with our children. (1980's)
OPPOSITE MIDDLE: Me with my children (1990's)
OPPOSITE BOTTOM: With Clive (1990's)

Clive & I with our granddaughter Emily (My Little Princess).

With my grandson James on a trip out to London – he is the apple of my eye.

TOP LEFT: My Mum & Dad.
TOP RIGHT: My treasured Roddy Doll (2021)
BELOW: My precious little dog Gambit.

A treasured photo of me and my dad on a trip
out to Busy Park.

I would like to say an extra thank you to my son Adam, who has worked extremely hard, and had put on hold his own writing of his books to help me put together and design this book.

I am truly grateful and could not have done this without you.

Printed in Great Britain
by Amazon

12853035R00129